From Orphan To Physician – The Winding Path

From Orphan To Physician – The Winding Path

Chun-Wai Chan, MD

Healthy Life Press
Orlando, Florida

Published by:
Healthy Life Press, 2603 Drake Drive, Orlando, FL 32810
www.healthylifepress.com

Cover design by Judy Johnson
Cover photo © Anduca | Dreamstime.com

Printed in the United States of America

Library of Congress Cataloging-in-Publication Data
Chan, Chun-Wai
From Orphan to Physician - The Winding Path

ISBN 978-1-939267-18-4

1. Autobiography; 2. Christian Living; 3. Inspiration

Dedication

This book is dedicated to my wife, Jade.

Jade, words cannot begin to describe my deep love for you and appreciation that comes from the bottom of my heart.

Thank you so much for your selfless love to me and to our children, your understanding of my shortcomings, your patience in waiting for God's timing, your prayers behind the scene, as well as your support and encouragement in everything that I do.

You are my most precious gift from God. I feel so blessed to have you as my life companion, as we walk through the winding path of life together.

Acknowledgements

There are so many people to whom I want to express my appreciation for their help in various stages of my life. I am sure that I will forget to mention someone. If I do, please forgive me and please be reassured that you are appreciated.

Thanks to my mother who bore me and raised me in a most difficult time. Her perseverance to live on has taught me many valuable lessons.

Thanks to Rev. Palmer who got me off the streets of Hong Kong and placed me in the orphanage.

Special thanks to Mrs. Doris Hawkins for sponsoring me in the orphanage. Because of her, I was able to have food, shelter, and education, at a critical time when I needed help the most. Furthermore, it was her unconditional love that led me to understand the agape love of God.

Thanks to Shing-Lam Chu, John Law, and other friends with whom I grew up in the orphanage. They are so much a part of my life.

Thanks to Rev. Peter Chiu, son of the superintendent of the orphanage, who led me to the Lord.

Thanks to Ms. Alice Lan, Ms. Vera Shen, Rev. Wai Kun Yu, Rev. Peter Lai, Dr. Peter Chiu, Rev. Simon Kang and other teachers at Bethel High School who were instrumental in shaping and molding me to become who I am today.

Thanks to my grandfather who persisted in finding us, and went to the trouble to get us visas to come to the United States.

Special thanks to Rev. Verent Mills, who treated me like his own son, and showed me a father's love, which I had never experienced.

Thanks to Dr. and Mrs. Don and Muriel Strum who continue to be my role models of loving and caring for others without asking for anything in return.

Thanks to Dr. Wei-Jen Huang, and Rev. Albert Lam for mentoring us.

Thanks to brothers and sisters at various churches for the joy of growing spiritually and serving together.

Special thanks to my children, Jamie, Janice, and Verent, for their love and understanding, despite all my shortcomings.

Finally, I want to thank Don and Muriel Strum and Victor Lai for reading my manuscript over and over again, and giving valuable suggestions. Without their help and encouragement, this book could not have been a reality.

Publisher's Note:

The author is donating net proceeds from the sale of this book to support the work of the Children's Garden Foundation, information about which is included in the back section of the book.

Foreword by Dr. Huang

If someone is wounded by the storms of life but experiences God's healing, he would understand the pain of others, and know how to comfort and encourage those who suffer from the turmoil of life.

I met Chun-Wai and Jade in 1993 at a family camp sponsored by Chinese Family For Christ, Inc. Since then we have had many opportunities to serve together in couple's ministry through which we have become good friends.

From Chun-Wai's life, we can see many touching and admirable experiences from which we can learn. For example, his family was so poor when he was little that he could only afford to watch children, dressed in crisp uniforms, going to school. Yet he was so eager to learn that he stood outside the school fence for hours each day, observing the teacher in the classroom and learning to write in the dirt.

When both his father and brother died because they had no money to buy medicine, his mother tricked him into entering the orphanage in order to survive. Little Chun-Wai had experienced loneliness, helplessness, and the pain of abandonment. The deep emotional wounds caused him to not trust anyone. On top of that, he was bullied by the bigger boys. Under these circumstances he learned to fight back and became mischievous.

But God turned Chun-Wai's life around and he learned to love and give love to others. When he realized that his extremely trying childhood experiences had a lot to do with his difficulty in controlling his negative emotions, he had the courage to face the problem head-on, and has been constantly trying to improve himself. It is admirable that, as a father, he was willing to humble himself and apologize to his children when he knew he was wrong.

One can see many of God's miracles in Chun-Wai. He survived many times "against all odds." God has given him wisdom, talents, and perseverance to accomplish much. He turned his hurts into strength. He has power but does not abuse it. He uses his influence to bring about improved healthcare for the needy. He and his wife are particularly tender toward those who are hurt emotionally, and they are constantly learning in order to know how best to help others.

I am so happy that Chun-Wai wrote this book to tell others about the amazing evidence of God's grace in his life. May those who read it feel God's love, comfort, encouragement, and healing.

Dr. Wei-Jen Huang,
Professor of Clinical Psychology,
Northwestern University School of Medicine,
Chicago, Illinois

Foreword by Rev. Lai

Before Jesus ascended to heaven, He told his disciples to bear witness for Him. Therefore, every Christian has a mission: to witness to others about the wonderful work of Jesus in his or her life. Some witness through songs, oral testimonies, or books. Some witness through their talent, money, or even their lives. The method may be different, but the purpose is the same: to bring people to Christ through which God is glorified.

In this book, Dr. Chan describes how his family escaped to Hong Kong, how they survived in utter poverty, and how he went from being an orphan to graduating from Harvard Medical School and becoming a cardiologist. The writing is fluent, easy to read and to understand. The sequence of events is realistic, emotionally moving, spiritually touching, heart-warming, and thought provoking. The author repeatedly experienced God's miracles, enabling him to accomplish much. Yet he constantly hid himself and gave glory to God.

The book illustrates a truth that passes the test of time: a successful person must possess diligence, perseverance, humility, and other virtues. Most importantly, however, one must have faith in order to walk through life's winding path.

Dr. Chan is a very grateful individual. In today's society, it is increasingly difficult to find this kind of person. I was deeply moved by how he expressed gratitude to his sponsor who sent five dollars a month to help him, and to the missionary who helped him and his family. Furthermore, even though I taught him in junior high school for only a short period of time, the respect he has given me is very touching.

Our church and I have supported an orphanage for many years. The superintendent wrote a book, which is entitled "One Hundred and Twenty Stories." In the book she wrote the story of every child in the orphanage. Yes, our lives are stories. We can tell others about our lives orally or in writing, so that others can benefit and God is glorified.

When Dr. Chan sent me the manuscript, my wife and I read it over and over again, and we were blessed by it. We highly recommend this book. May you be richly blessed through reading it.

Rev. Peter Lai
Senior Pastor, emeritus
Truelight Presbyterian Church
Alhambra, California

Preface

Every time we have out-of-town guests visiting us, we like to take them to Yosemite National Park. To me it is one of the most beautiful national parks I have visited. The Yosemite Valley was carved by the melting glaciers in ancient times. Today there are dramatic waterfalls, massive granite domes, towering cliffs, giant sequoia trees, perfectly tranquil lakes, and mosaics of open meadows sprinkled with wildflowers, shrubs, and trees. Each time I visit Yosemite, the majestic scenery inspires me to appreciate God's wonderful creation and the minuteness of men in the midst of the grand scale of nature.

The drive up and through Yosemite from the south entrance can be challenging for those who are not familiar with the road because the road is carved through rock formations with many twists and turns. When you reach a sharp bend in the road, the path ahead is often obscured by jutting rocks. After an hour of going through all the twists and turns, you enter a long tunnel. At the end of the tunnel, you finally arrive at Inspiration Point. It is there where the most beautiful panoramic view of the entire Yosemite Valley awaits your visual enjoyment.

Life is pretty much like a winding path. There are many twists and turns, crossroads, and even dark tunnels in life. Going through it can be scary at times, because we don't see what is ahead. But God is our perfect Global Positioning System (GPS). He knows every twist and turn. In fact, He plans our lives that way so that through the turmoil we become "mature and complete, not lacking anything" (James 1:4). He will guide us through, if we let Him.

Those who do not know me that well know only that I graduated from Princeton and Harvard, and that I am the chief of cardiology and assistant physician-in-chief of a medical center. Usually people are very surprised when I tell them I grew up in an orphanage. Actually, I could not have survived my childhood without the help of many people. Furthermore, if God had not healed me, I would not be here today.

As I reflect on my life, I can see many twists and turns. The most comforting thing is that God chose me to be His child even before I knew Him. When I lost my earthly father, He stepped in to fill the void and become my heavenly Father. At different stages of my life, He sent different people to help me out. When I fell, He lifted me up. When I strayed from Him, He gently guided me back to the right path. When I was prideful, he disciplined me so that I learned to trust Him instead of myself. How wonderful is God's love, especially to orphans and widows!

I want to share my life story with others not because I am rich and famous, or that I have anything of which I can boast, but because I am convinced that God has a perfect plan for each of us. There is a reason He allows all the twists and turns, crossroads and tunnels in each of our lives.

My prayer is that this book will be an encouragement to you. When you reach a bend in the road and don't see what is ahead, do not be afraid. "Trust in the Lord with all your heart and lean not on your own understanding; in all your ways acknowledge him, and he will make your paths straight" (Proverbs 3:5-6). May God have all the glory and praise!

– Chun-Wai Chan, MD
March 2011

13

Chun-Wai Chan, MD

CONTENTS

Chun-Wai Chan, MD

CHAPTER 1

IT ALL BEGAN IN HONG KONG (1951–1959)

BORN IN A REFUGEE FAMILY

> *"My frame was not hidden from you when I was made in the secret place, when I was woven together in the depths of the earth. Your eyes saw my unformed body; all the days ordained for me were written in your book before one of them came to be"* (Psalm 139:15-16).

I believe that God is the Creator of the universe and all that is in it. He created heaven and earth. Of course, He also created me. Not only so, He predestined me to become His vessel for His purpose. Nevertheless, for the longest time I could not fathom why I was born into a poor family such as mine.

Shortly after World War II, civil war broke out in China. The Nationalist and Communist soldiers fought fiercely to gain control of the country. In 1949, the Nationalist Army was defeated and retreated to Taiwan. The People's Liberation Army took over the control of mainland China. Many landlords, wealthy business owners, and the educated fled to Hong Kong for fear of persecution by the Communists. As a result, Hong Kong was swamped with floods of refugees from China in the 1950s.

My father's family owned acres and acres of land along the shore of Haikou in Hainan Island. They had a thriving business collecting sea salt for processing into table salt, which was then a valuable commodity in inland China. However, my father was in the military of the nationalist government. Without a doubt, he would be a prime target for persecution by the Communists.

Therefore, my parents, along with my older brother and sister, reluctantly left Hainan Island for Guangzhou in October 1950. As they arrived at the train station, they found that the station was overcrowded with people who were also trying to leave China. When they elbowed their way to the ticket counter, they discovered that all the tickets for the train to Hong Kong were completely sold out. They were panic-stricken and did not know what to do next. Luckily, through some connections, they were able to obtain four tickets through the black market and took the last train from Guangzhou to Hong Kong. They were hoping that when the dust settled and the situation became more stable, they could return home. They never thought that their dream of returning to the homeland would fade so quickly.

Life in Hong Kong at that time was a lot harder than they had expected it to be. The tremendous influx of refugees overwhelmed Hong Kong's social system. Jobs were scarce. Housing was in short supply. Most of the refugees, including my parents, had left all their possessions in China and did not know anyone in Hong Kong. My parents had only enough money to rent a small room in a wooden shed in the shanty town of Kowloon Zai.

Kowloon Zai in those days was a slum area filled with makeshift wooden huts of varying sizes. The shed my family lived in was a two-storied, U-shaped, wooden frame structure with roof and walls consisting of merely scraps of cardboard and rusty sheets of metal nailed together. Thirty-two refugee families lived in this building. Each family had just one room that measured about six by eight feet. At the end of each hallway of this U-shaped building there was a makeshift kitchen with two wood-burning stoves. Eight families took turns using this cooking facility, which was a constant source of conflict.

There was no bathroom facility, electricity, or running water in the building. Every morning each family carried water from a nearby creek about a hundred feet away. Water was then stored in plastic buckets for use for the rest of the day. But the creek was also used for washing and cleaning. For sanitary reasons, everyone observed the unspoken rule that cleaning of the portable commode had to be done a little farther downstream. Even so, water from the creek was contaminated because the creek flowed very slowly most of the time.

Each family had a small kerosene lamp as the source of lighting at night. Consequently, fire was a constant hazard in this shantytown. Each winter many buildings similar to ours burned to the ground, sometimes leveling the entire area. Therefore, all belongings had to be bundled up at all times so that it would be easy to grab them and run in case of fire.

Seasonal rains and typhoons brought their share of danger

19

and discomfort. As the roof was made out of sheet metal, it was very noisy when it rained, and containers were needed to collect water that leaked through the roof. When typhoons threatened the area every summer, the building had to be evacuated for safety reasons. The owner of the restaurant across the street was nice enough to let us use his facility as shelter whenever typhoons hit the area. Frequently, the cardboard and sheet metal would be ripped by the storm. Everyone had to help scavenge more cardboard and sheet metal discarded by nearby factories to put the roof and walls together again.

My father struggled to find work to feed the family. He did not have an easily marketable skill. Several attempts to start an import/export business venture failed miserably. My mother had been an elementary school teacher in China. Her teaching credentials, however, did not apply in Hong Kong. Therefore, she was unable to find a teaching job. Instead, she did embroidery work at home to supplement the family income.

My family, which consisted of my parents, my older sister, and my brother was at the bottom of the poverty level when I was born. We crowded in the little six-by-eight-foot room, not knowing if we would have enough money to buy food each day. Usually dinner was merely white rice with some salt or soy sauce. When rice was low, they would make it into diluted porridge so that it would go further.

In fact, my parents were so poor that they could not afford to buy milk to feed me. Instead, my mother fed me rice water mixed with a little bit of sugar. After awhile, my whole body was swollen from lack of protein. My mother took me to Kwong Wah Hospital (a government hospital for the poor). After waiting in line all day I was finally seen by the doctor and was diagnosed with kidney failure from severe malnutrition. From that point on, no matter how hard they had to work, my parents always made sure that, by the end of the day, they had money to buy condensed milk for me.

Two years later my younger brother was born, adding to the financial burden of the family. As a result, my parents had to work long hours each day to make ends meet. My father seldom came home before dark. I was usually fast asleep by the time he returned from work. At times I woke up in the middle of the night and would find him still working at the desk. In fact, my best recollection of my father is of the long shadow of his back cast by the flickering light from the kerosene lamp.

ACCEPTANCE BY GOVERNMENT SCHOOL

> *"Although the Lord gives you the bread of adversity and the water of affliction, your teachers will be hidden no more; with your own eyes you will see them"* (Isaiah 30:20).

There was no compulsory education in Hong Kong in the 1950s. I did not have the luxury of going to school because we were poor. Most of my childhood was spent playing in the dirt and with makeshift toys. I caught ladybugs in the field of a nearby high school, and spiders and cockroaches around the building where we lived. The spiders were the kind that would fight when faced off against each other in a tight compartment. I would build little boxes out of succulent plants for the spiders to live in and for staging fights. The cockroaches were huge, some as big as four inches long. I would tie threads around their bodies and run along with them as

21

they flew.

My favorite time of the day was after supper when all the kids in the neighborhood would show up at the playground of the high school nearby. We usually flew kites, played soccer, jumped ropes, or played hopscotch, almost always well into the evening until it was completely dark outside. Our kites were made of newspaper and bamboo strips glued together using rice paste. Some kids would go so far as to coat their kite lines with ground-up, broken glass, which allowed them to cut another's line if they should cross.

Watching building construction was by far my favorite pastime. I was fascinated by the heavy machinery that was used to pound steel beams into the ground for foundation support. Equally fascinating was the erection of bamboo scaffolding around the buildings by the skillful workers. The taller the building, the taller the scaffolding became. Some buildings were over ten stories tall, yet the workers climbed up and down and all around the bamboo scaffolding as if they were walking on the ground! Next to my home they were building the refugee resettlement housing funded by the United Nations, and Maryknoll Elementary School, a Catholic school. I actually watched the construction of these two projects from start to finish.

When the school opened, I used to envy the children filing into the school each morning. Every student was dressed in a crisp school uniform. How I wished I could attend school! Each day I would stand for hours outside the school fence watching all that was going on inside. I later found a spot from which I could peek and eavesdrop into the classroom. I tried to take in as much as possible what the teacher was teaching. I would then practice writing on the dirt, since I had no paper or pencil.

Later the Salvation Army opened a library not too far from our neighborhood. I started going to the library every day to read books on my own. Before long, the librarian learned about my family situation, that my parents were too poor to send me to school. Impressed with how eager I was to learn, she was extremely helpful. She guided me in the choice of books I should read and taught me new words whenever she was not busy.

My diligence finally paid off. A new government school was built about two to three miles from my home. Acceptance into the school required an entrance examination since there were too many children for the spaces available. My father took me to the new school for the entrance examination. A few weeks later he came home unusually early with a little package wrapped in beautiful wrapping paper.

"This is for you," he said, handing me the package.

"What is it?" I asked curiously.

"Open it and see," he urged.

I carefully unwrapped the package, making sure the shiny wrapping paper was not damaged so that it could be used again. I was overjoyed when I saw that it was a beautiful pencil – the very first pencil I had owned in my life!

He went on to explain, "Over three thousand children were competing for a hundred or so first grade places. You scored the third highest! This is your reward for doing so well in the entrance examination."

My mother added, "Pretty soon you will be able to go to school. Study hard so that our hope in you is not in vain. One day you will rise above everyone else." I would never forget their affirmation and encouragement.

My mother wanted me to become a doctor. This had little to do with goals of wealth or reputation. She simply wanted to make sure that in case I was ever uprooted and forced to flee to another country, I would have a marketable skill. She believed that medicine was the only profession that would provide protection for me and my family should the need arise.

Indeed, my parents were very proud of me. Even though tuition was only three dollars a month, it was an extra financial burden for them. Nevertheless, they were happy to work harder and longer hours to support my education.

My parents could not afford to buy me a school uniform, so my mother made the uniform herself. The quality and workmanship, understandably, were not as good as those ordered through the school. She also deliberately made my uniform several sizes larger so that it would last longer. It did not bother me. I was just happy to be able to go to school.

I walked to school every day since I had no money to pay for the bus fare. It took about an hour to walk each way. Because of the long journey, I learned to manage my time efficiently early on. While walking, I would review my schoolwork and force myself to recite the lessons. By the time I got to school, I usually would have learned the material by heart.

Unfortunately, the problem with walking such a long distance to school was the unpredictable nature of the weather during rainy seasons. Frequently I would become soaking wet walking to or from school if it rained all of a sudden and I had not brought a raincoat. Once, school had to end early because of a fast-approaching typhoon. I waited for a long time for my parents to come pick me up. When most of the people were gone, I realized that they probably would not be coming after all. I then walked back home by myself in the midst of the storm. At that time I was a small and skinny six-year-old. The strong wind actually knocked me down several times as I walked home. Fortunately, several adults let me hold onto them as we walked through the storm and I was able to make it home safely.

BECOMING AN ORPHAN

> *"In this you greatly rejoice, though now for a little while you may have had to suffer grief in all kinds of trials" (1 Peter 1:6).*

Less than a year after I started school, my younger brother died of infection from an insect bite. Within the same year my father passed away from infectious hepatitis. These unfortunate events would not have happened had we been able to pay for the necessary medical care. Shortly afterward, my father's small business was quickly taken over by creditors. At that time my younger sister was two years old and my mother was pregnant with my second younger sister.

Without the breadwinner in the family, once again we were literally thrown back into the mean streets of Hong Kong. My mother couldn't pay for my tuition even though it was just three dollars per month. As a result, I was unable to go to school anymore. I didn't understand. Why would God allow terrible things to happen to us one after another? I thought God was a loving God – at least that was what I had been told in Sunday school.

Until then we were attending a small church which was founded by my father. Church members were very concerned with our situation. They had vowed to collectively support and help my family. But in those days everyone else was struggling as well. My mother cried every day, as she struggled so hard trying to feed a family of six all by herself. With small children at home, the only job she could do was piecework embroidery from home. Having to work practically every available minute, my mother had to stop attending church.

Rev. Palmer, an American missionary who also attended our church, was indeed an angel sent by God. He continued to keep in touch with us from time to time. At times my mother did not have enough money to pay the rent. She had to swallow her pride and ask Rev. Palmer to help out. He was such a kind and generous person. Often he would also give my mother a few dollars extra so that she could buy some food for us.

Later on, an old acquaintance of my father opened a canvas shoe factory. He suggested my mother buy a sewing machine so that she could work from home. But where could she get the money? Again, Rev. Palmer came to our rescue. He loaned my mother the money to buy a sewing machine — the kind with a cast-iron foot pedal. With this machine she was able to work from home, sewing the top portion of canvas shoes.

With the sewing machine available at home, making canvas shoes became a family affair. Each day my brother and I would take a long bus ride to the factory to get the raw materials for our mother. My sisters would help with preparation for the sewing. The finished products would be carried back in exchange for piecework wages. When my second younger sister was born, my mom had to put her in Fanling Babies Home because she just could not make enough money to feed one more child.

Unfortunately, there were too many refugees wanting the same work. At times there was no work at all! It was not uncommon that we would go to bed hungry. The following day we would try our luck again to see if we could get some material to take back home for our mother to work on. When we did not have money to buy food, we would go to rice shops and offer to sweep the floors for them in the evenings. We were hoping to collect the rice that had spilled onto the floor during the day. We had to take out each grain of rice among the garbage we swept up so that we could make some porridge out of it.

Our meager existence went on for quite a few months until we learned that a soup kitchen had just opened up on the other side of the hill. On the days we did not have money to buy food, my brother and I would go to the soup kitchen and wait in line for several hours to get some soup and rice. The food was obviously not appetizing by any standard. Nonetheless, it filled our stomachs so we did not have to go to bed hungry.

Usually those who waited in line at the soup kitchen were women. We, two little boys, eventually attracted the attention of the staff. One of the female staff members was very sympathetic to our struggle to survive. She would give us extra portions and let us take some rice home for the rest of the family so that they would not go to bed hungry. With the help from the soup kitchen, we were able to carry on, or so we thought.

Chun-Wai Chan, MD

CHAPTER 2

ORPHANAGE UPBRINGING (1959–1969)

ENTERING FAITH-LOVE HOME

"I will not leave you as orphans; I will come to you"
(John 14:18).

After living in utter poverty for quite awhile, it was evident that my mother could not support a family of five on her own. But God never forsook us. When it seemed that we had come to the end of the road, God prepared a way out for us. Through Rev. Palmer I was placed in an orphanage. At that time Christian Children's Fund (CCF) operated five orphanages in Hong Kong. I was placed in the one called Faith-Love Home.

Christian Children's Fund (CCF) was originally called China's Children Fund. It was established in 1937 in Richmond, Virginia. Its mission was to save Chinese orphans who lost their parents from war or famine. At that time, a young man by the name of Verent Mills gave up his comfortable life in Canada, went to Qingyuan, Guangdong, at age eighteen and became a missionary. There he eventually established nine churches, as well as a Bible school to train local pastors.

The war and famine created thousands of orphans in the Siyup area of Guangdong. Rev. Mills took them in one by one. When the Japanese army advanced to the Guangdong area, he risked his life, climbed over rugged mountain ranges, and brought more than seven hundred orphans to safety. Christian Children's Fund supported his work. After the Communist Party took over China, he left China and went to Hong Kong where he established five orphanages and over twenty rooftop schools in various refugee resettlement areas. These afforded orphans and refugee children food, shelter, and a chance to obtain an education.

As there were so many children in Hong Kong needing help at that time, Christian Children's Fund was forced to make a choice. A decision was made to accept only children between the ages of six and ten to the orphanages so that they could concentrate their resources to make a positive impact in those lives. I was eight years old then and the only child in the family who was qualified to go to Faith-Love.

I remember my mom trying to tell me that there was a boarding school where I could attend school each day. Even though I did not like the idea of leaving the family, the thought of having a chance to attend school again was very appealing.

It was springtime when my brother and mother took me to Faith-Love Home. We took the train to Fanling, a small town in the New Territories. As soon as we got off the train, we were greeted by a fleet of bicycle peddlers who offered to take us to the destination for a fee. My mother initially tried to negotiate with them. She finally decided to walk to the orphanage, instead, to save money. It took us about an hour to walk there. I really enjoyed seeing the countryside with rice paddies everywhere, and the entire route was lined with eucalyptus trees. When the soft wind blew, we could smell the fragrance from those trees. After crossing a river and cutting through a village, we finally arrived at the gate of Faith-Love Home.

We were greeted at the gate by a teacher who took us to the office. After filling out the proper paperwork, the teacher asked a boy of my age to give me a tour of the home. Compared to our living conditions at home, this school was a luxury indeed. The dormitories, dining hall, classrooms, and infirmary were all built with concrete and granite. There was also a basketball court, a badminton court, and a playground with swings, slides, and seesaws. I couldn't wait any longer and started immediately playing with my newfound friends.

Apparently my mother and brother left while I was taking the tour. When I found out they were gone, I was scared. This was the first time in my young life I had been away from home. I did not know how I could survive without my family. At the same time, I was puzzled and felt abandoned because I did not understand why my mother would leave me in a strange place without saying goodbye. Later on, I found out that it was not a boarding school but rather an orphanage. I felt cheated.

I was angry at my mother. How could she do this to me? Why did she decide to put me, and not my brother or sisters, in an orphanage? Had I done something wrong to cause her to abandon me like that? All these questions bothered me for a long time because I could not find a good explanation. This had a profound impact on my trust of others, and it took me a long time to overcome it.

My first week in the orphanage was miserable. I didn't dare cry in front of the other children. Rather, I hid myself underneath the staircase at the back of the auditorium, sobbing for hours during the first few days. One day I longed for my mother so much that I mistakenly called the superintendent's wife, who was also my teacher, "Mom." I was so embarrassed afterward because the other children laughed at my mistake.

A week later Rev. Palmer and my mother came to visit me and to take me home for the weekend. I was all too happy to be home, enjoying every minute with my brother and my sisters. I especially enjoyed taking care of my younger sister who was four at that time. I even promised her that I would take care of her and would not leave her again.

But the weekend went by very fast. When it was time for me to return to Faith-Love, I told my mother that I didn't want to go back. Somehow she persuaded me to go with her to the bus terminal. She placed me on the front row seat behind the bus driver. Sitting next to me was a middle-aged lady who happened to be getting off at the same stop, the town of Fanling. My mother paid the lady some money and asked her to hire a pedicab for me when we got off at Fanling. As my mother was stepping off the bus and walking away, I burst into tears and started running off the bus.

"If you want to study at all, you have no other choice but to go back to Faith-Love," my mother explained.

She took me back onto the bus. She waited until the bus driver started the engine, then swiftly handed the lady my suitcase and ran off the bus just before the door closed behind her. I cried for her through the window, but she turned her back and started walking away. My vision was blurred from the tears as I watched her long, skinny shadow, cast by the setting sun, gradually disappearing in the distance. I sobbed until I fell asleep. By the time I awakened, the bus had just pulled into the town of Fanling. The bus driver opened the door and called out, "Fanling Marketplace!" Instinctively, I stepped off the bus. It was already nightfall. I could not recognize the place at all! The lady who had been sitting next to me also got off the bus. I fully expected that she would come to me, hold my hand, and tell me that she would take me back to the orphanage. Instead she was turning the opposite direction. For a moment I thought she would just pocket my mother's money and disappear. The thought of being left alone was terrifying!

But she kept her promise. She went to the other street corner to call a bicycle peddler to come over. After talking to him and paying the fare, she told the peddler to take me to the orphanage. The peddler helped me hop on the back of his bicycle, and we began the journey into the darkness.

For the next twenty minutes I was completely overwhelmed by fear. The road was so poorly lit that I could not see where the peddler was headed. I also remembered my mother telling me time and again that there were child snatchers who would capture children and sell them as slaves. My heart was pounding hard as I tried to plan how I would jump off the bicycle and run away from the peddler and the child snatchers in case something bad happened.

Suddenly the bicycle came to a stop. I looked up and was relieved to see the familiar front gate of the school. I was never so happy to be back at the orphanage. From that point on I knew I had to accept my fate at the orphanage and make the most out of whatever my situation happened to be.

A year later, my mother remarried. Even though my step-

33

father was not rich by any standard, life for my family had significantly improved. They moved out of the shantytown and into an apartment. With my stepfather's connections, my older brother and sister were able to go back to school. My stepfather wanted to get me out of the orphanage. However, my mother decided to leave me there since it was free.

By then I had gotten used to the orphanage anyway. I was actually glad that my mother decided to keep me in the orphanage. Some of the neighborhood kids called me Yao-peng-zai, a derogatory term for an orphan boy whose mother was remarried. One time I was so mad at someone calling me Yao-peng-zai that I broke the door to the rooftop of the apartment building. I also didn't like the first and last name given to me by my stepfather. To this day, I still keep my family name.

Three times a year I was allowed to visit my family: Christmas, Chinese New Year, and summer recess. I did enjoy the brief stay in the apartment. The building was eight stories high, with a flat rooftop, and was located near the runway of the then Kai-Tak International Airport. The area was very noisy outside because of the frequent plane traffic. Nevertheless, I spent most of my time on that rooftop playing games with other kids and watching the planes take off and land. I was fascinated by the sheer size of the jets and always wondered how it would feel to ride in one.

My mother told me that my grandfather was in the United States. At the age of eighteen he had gone to the United States as a laborer to earn money for his parents in China. Two years later he had come back to China to get married. After my aunt and my mother were born, he returned to the States to continue working and regularly sent money to my mother's family. Unfortunately, my mother had lost contact with him after World War II. Obviously, he didn't even know that my family had escaped to Hong Kong in 1950.

As I was watching the planes take off and disappear into the horizon, I frequently fantasized that some day I would travel to America to find my grandfather. I thought I could work hard and make a lot of money to send back to my mother so that she could live comfortably. Deep down, however, I knew this was only a fantasy. How could I find my grandfather in America when I didn't even know where he was living? Besides, with our economic situation, how could we ever afford the cost of traveling overseas? Getting an education in the orphanage was the best chance I had to get out of poverty.

LEARNING TO BE TOUGH

"You hear, O Lord, the desire of the afflicted; you encourage them, and you listen to their cry, defending the fatherless and the oppressed, in order that man, who is of the earth, may terrify no more" (Psalm 10:17-18).

Life in the orphanage was very regimented. Each morning we were awakened at 6:00 AM by the "bell"—a sound produced by using a metal clapper hitting a three-foot piece of railroad track hanging on a tree branch. Within fifteen minutes we were expected to finish making our beds, brushing our teeth, and washing our faces. We had a military-style morning drill before our breakfast, which was almost always porridge. After breakfast we had preassigned chores to do: washing dishes, sweeping floors, washing windows, or cleaning the school grounds. Morning assembly would follow before morning classes. Then we had lunch followed by more cleaning, afternoon classes, free time, and then dinner.

Dinner was always two vegetables with rice. We seldom had meat unless visitors were coming. Boys often did not have enough to eat. As a result, we frequently stole each other's food during the prayer time before we ate. Fistfights were inevitable when that happened.

After dinner, we had to wash up before evening homework time. The day ended with evening prayers, and lights were out by 9:00 PM. Punctuality was expected. Any time the "bell" sounded we were expected to stand at a preassigned spot in the courtyard, rain or shine. Tardiness greater than two minutes would result in standing in the courtyard while the others enjoyed their food.

While our schedule was regimented, it did allow for some personal time. In addition to studying and doing the routine chores, I picked up several hobbies. One of them was playing the harmonica and the Chinese flute. Around Christmas, my sponsor (the person who supported me by contributing five dollars each month to CCF) sent me five dollars. I spent the money on these two instruments. One of my schoolmates taught me the basics, and I just practiced on my own hour after hour until my mouth hurt. When the teacher organized a flute ensemble, I was not selected because "my fingers were too short." However, I was persistent and kept on begging him to let me in. Finally, he let me audition for the ensemble. He was amazed at my ability to play, and I was accepted right away.

Even though our daily routine was structured, supervision was lacking. There were only eight teachers for 168 children, far too few to provide any significant individual attention for the growth and development of each child. Consequently, we were pretty much left alone most of the time to deal with our own interpersonal conflicts.

During my first year in the orphanage, I was routinely bullied by the older boys. One day I was watching them playing basketball. For no reason at all one of them threw the ball at my face and broke my front tooth. With blood coming out of my month, I burst into tears, but no one was there to help or comfort me.

Another time I made a toy boat out of discarded Popsicle sticks. A bully snatched the toy from me, broke it, and stomped on it until it was no longer recognizable as a boat.

"Why did you break my boat?" I asked, my voice quavering.

"I just felt like it," he replied, then walked away, laughing.

I didn't cry. There was no use crying because no one was there to comfort me or speak up on my behalf.

Still another time I was washing clothes near a sink. Another big bully falsely accused me of removing his clothes from the sink. When I told him that the sink had been empty when I arrived, he hit me on my back so hard that I was knocked to the ground. I pretended that I was unconscious. He got scared and ran away.

Over time I learned that in order to protect myself I had to be aggressive and mean. One day another boy pushed me around for no reason. I did not know how I got the courage and strength. I knocked him to the ground, sat on top of him, and kept hitting him on his face until he started to bleed from his nose. After that he didn't take advantage of me anymore. After winning a few fistfights, a group of kids started calling me "big brother Wai." Unintentionally, I had formed a gang at the young age of nine.

Without proper guidance from the teachers, we did all sorts of mischievous things. We would sneak into nearby family farms to steal chicken eggs. We would chase away the ducks at the river not far from the orphanage and snatch their eggs. We would even go out to the market and steal things from the street vendors. We used foul language uninhibitedly. We took advantage of the younger kids, called them names, punished them, and made them our slaves through intimidation. Nevertheless, all the temporary excitement from being mischievous could not fill a certain void inside my heart.

Because I did not spend time studying, my grades went downhill. I was a headache for the teachers. But for some reason, they were especially lenient to me. In one incident I broke someone's foot during an altercation. Much to everyone's surprise, the teacher on duty did not punish me at all. A few days later, the uncle of the boy came to the orphanage and demanded that the teacher hand me over to him. The principal's wife hid me in her quarters until he left the orphanage.

LIFE-CHANGING CONVERSION

"In his heart a man plans his course, but the Lord determines his steps" (Proverbs 16:9).

Despite how lenient the teachers were to me, I did not appreciate it. Instead, I was constantly being mischievous behind the teachers' backs. In order to prevent us from causing trouble outside, the orphanage had a very strict rule that no one was allowed to leave the orphanage without permission from the teacher on duty. Failure to obey this rule would result in severe punishment. But sometimes, life in the orphanage was too routine and boring. Some of us were always looking for any excuse to leave the orphanage to find something more exciting to do outside.

One weekend there was an evangelistic meeting at a church in town. "Wow! This is a great chance to get out of the orphanage and do something fun," several of my buddies suggested.

"What do you have in mind?" I asked.

"Sneak into the theater to watch a movie for free," one said. "We can hold onto the clothing of some adults and pretend we are their children. We can bend our knees when walking in so that we look shorter," he added.

"Snatch peanuts from the street peddlers outside the movie theater," another countered. "It is the easiest thing to do. Look! Two of you stage a fight in front of the street vendors. While everyone is distracted, I can snatch several bags of peanuts and then we can all share our bounty."

After listening to them, I said, "They are good ideas, but we have to get permission from the teacher in order to go out."

So I made the request on behalf of the group to attend the evangelistic meeting. The teacher on duty was impressed with how eager we were to listen to the gospel. As expected, she granted our request.

As we were walking to town, we plotted what we would do next. When we passed by the church, I was attracted by the beautiful singing coming out of the sanctuary. We decided to walk up to the church building. We stepped on a rock, peeked in through the window, and found that the beautiful singing was coming from the choir. I thought that one day I might be able to sing in the choir too. Before long, the speaker, who was an American but was preaching in near-perfect Cantonese, spotted us.

"Come on in, boys. Jesus is waiting for you," he said, invitingly.

Everyone turned their head in our direction. Then two

middle-aged ladies came out of the sanctuary and invited us in. At that point, we had no choice but to follow them inside. I could not remember what the message was about. But when the speaker called people to accept Jesus Christ, my heart was pounding really hard. Though I did not raise my hand, the seed of the gospel had been sown. After the meeting was over, I told my buddies that we should not steal anymore, and we returned to the orphanage empty-handed.

Several weeks later, an evangelistic meeting was held at the orphanage. The speaker was the principal's son, who was graduating from seminary. This time I couldn't help but pay attention to the sermon, because the whole sermon was about me! I realized that my disobedient, sinful nature would not allow me to do good unless Jesus Christ came into my heart. When the speaker invited people to come forward, I was the first one walking to the podium. I accepted Jesus Christ as my personal Savior that day and was baptized on Easter Sunday, 1962.

BEGINNING A NEW LIFE

> *"Therefore, if anyone is in Christ, he is a new creation; the old has gone, the new has come!"*
> *(2 Corinthians 5:17).*

Thereafter my life took a one-hundred-eighty-degree turn. All the things I had thought were exciting to do were no longer of any interest to me. Also, my anger and bitterness were replaced by the love of God and the joy of knowing that Jesus was there for me and would take good care of me. I began to pray to God whenever things bothered me, and I always felt better afterward.

For example, one time a classmate was teasing me about my broken tooth. Instead of striking back, I prayed and asked God to punish her. Then I realized that I shouldn't be so vindictive. So I prayed again during recess. I then felt better. By the end of the recess, she came over and apologized!

Moreover, with enlightenment from the Holy Spirit, I began to distinguish between right and wrong. I felt strongly that once I had become a Christian I could not continue my old way of living anymore. I returned everything I had stolen to the original owners. I asked for forgiveness and expressed my willingness to receive punishments. There were no more fistfights or foul language. Instead of taking advantage of the younger kids, I offered to help them any way I could. One day I noticed a kid who had really long fingernails because he didn't have a nail clipper. I offered to cut his nails, but he was very skeptical of my intentions. After I gave him my nail clipper so that he could cut them himself, he realized that I did not intend to harm him. We then became friends.

I wrote to my sponsor to tell her that I had become a Christian. She was overjoyed. She sent me five dollars which I used to buy a Bible, just for myself. I would wake up at about 4:00 AM each day, and read my Bible. I also devoted most of my free time to studying instead of being mischievous. I began to excel in school, obtaining near perfect scores on every test. At first, my teacher thought that I was cheating. During one test, he deliberately stood right next to me for the entire test. After I got another perfect score on the test, he was satisfied that I did not cheat to get a perfect score.

"What made you change from a naughty boy to a good student?" he asked curiously.

"I became a Christian," I replied.

Then I proceeded to tell him what had happened. He was

not totally convinced. Nonetheless, he was happy because I was no longer a headache to him.

Under the guidance of our Bible teacher, we enjoyed many organized group activities at the orphanage. First, we founded the Junior Fellowship. Besides having fellowship meetings every Saturday evening, we organized many activities including biking, hiking, fishing, and camping trips. We also started a photography club, and a gardening club to grow our own vegetables. We even put together drama and acrobatic performances for the Christmas rally, an annual Christmas gala celebrated with all the other CCF orphanages in Hong Kong.

I began to take on leadership duties. I learned to lead singspiration as well as be the moderator for the Sunday worship services. In addition, each summer I went to Lantau Island where selected students from each orphanage were brought together to experience leadership training. I did not know at the time that God was preparing me for the future.

When I graduated from elementary school, I was supposed to go to Children's Garden, a much larger orphanage with high school facilities. However, the principal of the orphanage really wanted some of us to stay around and help care for the younger children. He persuaded CCF office staff to allow seven of us to attend the high school in town and then return to Faith-Love after school to help run the after-school activities.

A semester later, we were transferred to Bethel High School in Kowloon. Bethel High School was part of the Bethel Biblical Seminary. It was relocated from Shanghai to Hong Kong in 1950. One of the distinctive features of the school was its emphasis on holistic character development in addition to academic excellence. Bible classes and Scripture memorization were required of all students throughout junior high and high school. Every Wednesday we had praise and worship services. The principal, the dean, and several teachers chose not to take any salary from the school. Instead, the school provided them with room and board and money to buy two sets of clothes per year. They dedicated their lives to serving God by serving students. To me this was most admirable.

Faith-Love was quite a distance from Bethel High School. Traveling back and forth took several hours each day. A typical day would involve getting up at 5:00 AM, walking forty-five minutes to the train station to catch the first train to Kowloon, and then taking a bus from the train station to school. When returning in the afternoon, we frequently fell asleep on the train. Amazingly we always managed to wake up just before the train pulled into the town of Fanling.

I really wanted to save time on my daily commute by riding a bicycle instead of walking to and from the train station. But how could I get the money to buy a bicycle? I came up with the idea of working part-time on Saturdays since school was only a half-day on Saturdays. I then prayed that God would help me find a part-time job. My prayer was answered! I found a part-time job cleaning the stairs of the teachers' quarters at Bethel. With the money saved, I bought a used bicycle, which proved to be extremely helpful.

The money I saved not only provided me the convenience of biking, but also the opportunity to learn to play the violin. The superintendent's second son was an excellent violinist. He played for the Hong Kong Philharmonic Orchestra. After listening to him practicing his violin night after night, I became very interested in the instrument. However, at that time in Hong Kong, violin lessons were very expensive and generally limited to children of wealthy families. As an orphan, I knew my desire to learn to play the violin was not realistic.

43

However, I thought I should at least give it a try. So I asked him if he would teach me to play the violin.

"You have to have a violin before I can teach you," he challenged me, thinking that I probably would not be able to come up with the money to buy a violin.

Several months later I handed him the thirty dollars for a student-model violin. Impressed with how hard I had to work each Saturday to save money for the violin, he agreed to give me violin lessons. The lessons were free of charge, provided I would run errands for him.

I continued to do well academically, winning academic awards each semester. At the end of the eleventh grade I sat for the Hong Kong Secondary School Certificate Examination. Good grades were essential for admission to college. When the results were announced in the newspapers, I couldn't believe my eyes. I received top grades in all ten subjects!

A month later, my high school principal called me to her office. I was very nervous because I didn't know what to expect.

"Congratulations! You have been offered a full scholarship by the Board of Education to attend Chinese University of Hong Kong. Your tuition for the twelfth grade is also paid for," she said.

I was thrilled! CCF sponsored children through age seventeen only. This scholarship was really a godsend, allowing me to continue my education without having to worry about how to finance it. I originally wanted to go to medical school at Hong Kong University because I was fascinated by how different parts of the body worked together to maintain vital functions. Learning how science helped the understanding, diagnosis, and treatment of various diseases was something I wanted to pursue. However, I knew this was quite impossible because all my schooling was not within the British system, a prerequisite for taking the entrance examination to Hong Kong University. Since Chinese University of Hong Kong did not have a medical school at the time, my plan was to study chemistry there and become a high school teacher. But God had other plans in store for me.

Chun-Wai Chan, MD

CHAPTER 3

THE AMERICAN DREAM (1969–1971)

GOING TO AMERICA

"I will lead the blind by ways they have not known, along unfamiliar paths I will guide them; I will turn the darkness into light before them and make the rough places smooth. These are the things I will do; I will not forsake them" (Isaiah 42:16).

I had no clue that God had a different plan for me. All this time, my grandfather had been looking for us without success through the missing persons section of local newspapers in China. Fortunately, my granduncle came to Hong Kong to visit his family and learned that my family had relocated to Hong Kong in 1950. As soon as he went back to

47

the States, he told my grandfather about it. After establishing contact with us, my grandfather became a great help to our family financially. He also applied for visas for us to come to America. During the summer between my eleventh and twelfth grades, we went through the interview process for our immigration visas. In just a matter of months we would have to uproot ourselves one more time.

This was a dream come true! Since elementary school I had dreamed of traveling overseas. Realizing that I had been born poor, I did not have much hope that my dream would become real. Now the prospect of going to America was exciting to me. Knowing that I needed to learn more English, I enrolled myself in an evening English class taught by a missionary. In my spare time I started to memorize five words a day from a pocket dictionary. I also started to review science textbooks so that I would be familiar with scientific terms in English. Every chance I had, I would strike up conversations with American tourists visiting Hong Kong. By the end of summer, I had learned enough to read English newspapers and carry on simple conversations in English.

I had barely started back to school when the U.S. consulate notified us that our visas were approved. Unfortunately, visas for my older brother and sister were not granted at the same time because they were over eighteen. We were told that we had only ninety days to immigrate to the United States. So we spent the following two months busily packing and shipping our belongings, selling furniture, appliances, and bulky items, and saying goodbye to friends and relatives. This was a very emotional time for me. On the one hand it was sad to have to leave all my friends with whom I had grown up and who had become so much a part of my life. On the other hand, the excitement of going to America was so overwhelming that I was able to put aside the sadness, at least for the time being.

On Thanksgiving Day, November 27, 1969, with a combined total of thirty-five dollars in our pockets, we took a PanAm flight to New York. The first stop was Tokyo, Japan. We had not been told that we had to change planes in Tokyo. So when we landed in Tokyo and it was time to deplane, my family did not want to get off the plane. But I was curious about what a Japanese air terminal looked like. So I followed the rest of the passengers and walked into the terminal. I was thinking that in a few minutes I would be able to find my way back to the plane.

Wow! The Tokyo International Airport was the biggest building structure I had ever set foot on! I was fascinated by all the shops, displaying all kinds of merchandise that I didn't know existed. So I walked and walked until I realized that I was lost. I managed to find a stewardess who was nice enough to take me to the boarding gate for the next flight to New York. It was, however, a different gate from the one where I had deplaned.

Suddenly I realized that we had to change planes in Tokyo. For a moment I was very worried about my family who might still be sitting in the previous plane. Not understanding any English, they might not know what to do. But I was reassured that the stewardess helped my family board this plane directly without going through the terminal. So I waited patiently at the gate. But when it was time to board, I was denied boarding because I had not taken the boarding pass with me when I had exited the previous plane.

I was really scared. I didn't even have enough money with me for the next meal. What would I do alone in Japan? Also, what would happen to my family if they flew to New York

49

without me? I regretted walking out of the plane by myself and leaving my family behind. I began to blame myself for being so inconsiderate and absentminded.

Meanwhile, through the glass panel I saw that the propeller of the plane had started to turn. Just when they were ready to close the door of the plane, my stepfather got out of the plane and stood at the landing of the movable staircase, making all kinds of hand gestures to the stewardess, who was trying to drag him back into the plane. Finally, through an interpreter, the stewardess learned that I had not boarded. So she walked down the staircase, came to the gate, and verified that I was supposed to be on that plane. I was finally allowed to board and be reunited with my family.

The next stop was Fairbanks, Alaska. Peeking through the window, I saw snow for the first time in my life. Flakes of white, fluffy stuff were coming down so softly and slowly, lightly covering the building and ground of the airport. It was the most beautiful sight I had ever seen! Because of my earlier experience in Tokyo, I didn't dare deplane this time despite the stewardess urging us to get out of the plane to stretch. I was afraid I might get lost in the terminal again and miss the next flight.

After arriving at John F. Kennedy International Airport in New York, we had to go through a lengthy customs process. There I quickly learned that my English was not good enough to carry on a conversation with an average American. They spoke way too fast for me! The customs officer was very annoyed when I kept asking him to repeat what he said. Eventually he let us through after he realized that we were immigrants from Hong Kong.

I had never met my grandfather before, but I carried one of the pictures he had sent us. It was a picture of him in a three-piece suit standing next to a Cadillac and in front of a Chinese restaurant. My assumption was that as the owner of the restaurant and the Cadillac, he must be very rich. But when the taxi drove up to his apartment at Broadway and W. 108th Street, which was the edge of Harlem, I was very disappointed. The street was filthy. The building was at least a hundred years old. The apartment was dark and dingy. The hallway was narrow, and the door was double bolted for security. I quickly concluded that it must be a very unsafe area. All seven of us crammed into his tiny one-bedroom apartment. I couldn't understand why we had given up everything in Hong Kong only to live in a slum in America.

Becoming A Waiter

> *"Not only so, but we also rejoice in our sufferings, because we know that suffering produces perseverance; perseverance, character; and character, hope. And hope does not disappoint us, because God has poured out his love into our hearts by the Holy Spirit, whom he has given us"* (Romans 5:3-5).

Two days after our arrival in New York, my grandfather took me to his restaurant in Whitestone, Long Island. There I found out he was only a waiter, not the owner of the restaurant. He had actually owned a restaurant in Florida at one point but had lost it through gambling.

After a brief introduction to the manager and other staff, we went down to the basement. He handed me a waiter's jacket and started to teach me how to wait on tables. I could not believe it! I had given up a prestigious scholarship to come

51

to America, only to end up learning to be a waiter. My American dream was totally shattered!

Life as a waiter was very physically demanding. The day started with opening up the restaurant at 9:00 AM, sweeping the floor, washing the bathroom, making tea and coffee, and replenishing supplies, including table cloths, napkins, glasses, and utensils for each station, to salt, pepper, and soy sauce for each table. By 11:00 AM, customers would start coming in, and this kept us busy until about 3:00 PM when we could then have our lunch break. After a quick lunch, we had to help wrap wontons, egg rolls, and dumplings. By 5:00 PM, we had to get ready for dinner customers. On weekdays we stayed open until 11:00 PM and on weekends and holidays until 1:00 AM. By the time I walked back to the staff quarters, which were about fifteen minutes away, I was totally exhausted.

Besides long working hours, the work environment was less than desirable. Each waiter was assigned to wait on five tables. When the tables were full, it was quite tricky to attend to all the customers to their complete satisfaction. At times, some customers would complain that their food was not steaming hot. Since customers were always right, without saying a word, I then had to take the food back for the chefs to re-cook it. Invariably this would trigger very unpleasant verbal abuse by the chefs, including a significant amount of foul language. Yet no matter how upset I was, when I walked out of the kitchen and entered the dining area, I had to put on a big smile for the customers.

What bothered me most was the utter loneliness at night. After the restaurant was closed at night, the workers would visit a secret brothel where X-rated movies, gambling, or sex were offered for a price. God's protection came through His Word, which I had memorized when I was at Faith-Love as well as at Bethel. One of the most helpful verses was: "Above all else, guard your heart, for it is the wellspring of life" (Proverbs 4:23). Not once were they able to persuade me to go with them. Most of the time I walked back to the staff quarters alone. After washing up, I would lie in bed and stare at the ceiling until I fell asleep. How I wished I could go back to Hong Kong and be with my friends. Deep down, however, I knew that returning to Hong Kong was not an option.

GOING BACK TO SCHOOL

"God is our refuge and strength, an ever-present help in trouble" (Psalm 46:1).

At the lowest point of my spiritual life, however, God sent another angel to my rescue. One day someone passed out gospel tracts in the neighborhood of the restaurant and left some pamphlets by the porch of the staff quarters. When I retired to the quarters at night, I picked up the pamphlets. To my surprise, they were in Chinese! Inside the pamphlet was an article written by Rev. Simon Kang, who had been my geography and Bible teacher at Bethel High School in Hong Kong before he moved to New York in 1967. The next morning I called the phone number of the church listed in the pamphlet. A nice young lady helped me get in touch with Rev. Kang. During this critical period, Rev. and Mrs. Kang became my source of much-needed guidance.

Lying in bed one night, I realized that unless I improved my English, there would be no future for me. So I turned on the radio my grandfather had loaned me. Even though I did not understand a word from the broadcast because they spoke too fast, I left the radio on all night, even during my sleep, so that I would get used to the sound. I also deliberately awakened early in the morning so that I could learn English by watching the Sesame Street television program.

After about a month, my English had improved enough to carry on a conversation with customers in the restaurant. As a result, my income from tips steadily increased. But I could not see myself waiting on tables for the rest of my life. One evening I mustered up enough courage to tell my grandfather that I needed to quit work and go back to school.

"What did you just say?" he asked, because he could not believe his ears. He was shocked! He thought I was throwing away a golden opportunity to make good money.

"Work hard and save enough money so that one day you will be able to open a restaurant of your own," he said.

"But I don't want to work in a restaurant for the rest of my life," I argued.

"What's wrong with being your own boss? In America, money is everything. For Chinese the best way of making money is in the restaurant business," he continued.

I did not want to argue with him anymore. Eventually we reached a compromise: I would go to school during the week and work in the restaurant on weekends.

As it turned out, finding a school to accept me was no easy task. For the following weeks, I spent my days off visiting various high schools. Invariably I was told that the principal was too busy to talk to me. One secretary even told me that schools were under no obligation to accept anyone over seventeen. I was already eighteen at that time. I was afraid I might not be able to finish high school after all.

However, I was determined to find someone to talk to about my situation. I decided to stand in front of the principal's office at Louis Brandeis High School on 84th Street every week on my day off, waiting for the principal to see me. Finally my persistence paid off. Tired of seeing me outside the office each week, the assistant principal referred me to the Adult Evening School Program at Charles Evans Hughes High School on West 18th Street. The supervisor of the program, much to my surprise, was nice enough to review my transcripts from Hong Kong. He was quite impressed with my grades and my desire to go back to school. He told me that I should enroll in a better program than what he could offer me. So he wrote a note, placed it in a sealed envelope, and told me to take it to one of his friends at New York City's Board of Education.

The letter was addressed to a lady who was in charge of high school placement. After reading the note, she patiently listened as I told her how I had come to the States, worked in a restaurant, learned English through watching Sesame Street on TV, and how I wanted so desperately to further my education in spite of all the obstacles I was encountering. Impressed with my motivation and perseverance, she immediately placed me into the academic program of Charles Evans Hughes High School in March 1970. What a relief!

But transitioning back to high school was another matter. My English was tested to be at only the third grade level. So they assigned me to five different English classes, plus American history and economics. I studied very hard each day, usually well into the morning hours. On Fridays I would go back to the restaurant right after school and work there until Monday morning.

Several teachers were extremely helpful during my transition. They made me read the *New York Times* newspaper once a week. They took me to museums and theaters so that I could be exposed to American culture. As a result, I learned English quickly. I also forced myself to read one novel a week. By the end of that semester, my English had improved from third grade to the twelfth grade level. In addition, I took the New York State Regents Examinations on all other high school subjects without having taken the courses. I got excellent grades in all of them. I even became a student tutor for mathematics and science in the after-school-tutoring program. In January 1971 I graduated as the high school valedictorian.

Given my family's limited finances, my original plan was to attend City College of New York, which was tuition-free. But my college advisor challenged me. She said, "You should always aim for the moon. If you miss it, at least you might hit a star."

I thought long and hard about what she had said. Then I learned that all application fees would be waived for me because of our low family income. I felt that I had nothing to lose by applying to more competitive schools. The worst that could happen was that I might be rejected. So I also applied to Princeton, Cornell, Brown, University of Rochester, and New York University, even though I did not expect a positive response from them. Meanwhile, I attended Brooklyn College of the City University of New York as a high school student so that I would not be drafted by the army to go to Vietnam.

Finally my wait was over. On April 15, 1971, I received a registered letter from Princeton. "I am pleased to inform you . . . ," the letter began. My heart was pounding hard as I read on with anticipation. I could not believe it! I was not only accepted but also offered a full scholarship! I was so excited and filled with gratitude. I wondered how someone like me, with English not being my native language, could be accepted by the best university in America. Later I learned that my college advisor was able to convince Princeton's admissions committee to look beyond my SAT scores and judge my potential differently.

Looking back, I am convinced that God is especially kind and tender to orphans such as me. When I lost my earthly father, my heavenly Father stepped in and filled the void. From time to time, He would send different people into my life to help and guide me, even before I was aware of His presence.

Chun-Wai Chan, MD

CHAPTER 4

PRINCETON EXPERIENCE (1971–1975)

Experiencing Campus Life

> *"For I know the plans I have for you," declares*
> *the Lord, "plans to prosper you and not to harm*
> *you, plans to give you hope and a future" (Jere-*
> *miah 29:11).*

In August 1971 my mother and brother accompanied me to Princeton. As we entered the campus gate, my mind flashed back to the time they had taken me to the orphanage years ago. This time, however, was completely different. My mother was beaming with pride as we entered the beautiful campus. There were gothic style buildings with ivy-covered walls, a cathedral style chapel, massive libraries, and first class museums with collections of rare cultural treasures. The entire campus had manicured lawns, carefully trimmed trees, and interesting outdoor sculptures created by famous artists such as Picasso. Every dormitory had a courtyard, a dining hall, and a tennis court or other fitness facility. At the southern part of the campus was a beautiful, championship golf course. Next to it was a tranquil lake lined with willows and flowering shrubs. With our limited family income, my mother could not have imagined I would be attending such a prestigious and beautiful institution of higher learning.

Many of my classmates came from well-to-do families, including the daughter of the president of the Philippines, the great grandson of billionaire Rockefeller, and many children of the rich and famous. Their road to success was all mapped out for them early on in their lives. They were so affluent that very few of them needed financial assistance. For that reason, many scholarships were available. At that time, the Bank of China offered a full scholarship to Princeton but specified that only Chinese students born outside of the United States could apply. In the 1970s, very few Chinese students born outside of the United States were attending Princeton. Therefore, I was awarded the full scholarship without much competition.

Living on the Princeton campus was a brand-new experience for me. There I was introduced to a completely different way of living: sleeping on mattresses instead of bed-boards, using a washer and dryer instead of hand-washing my clothes, and using metal utensils instead of wooden chopsticks. It actually took me awhile to get used to the metallic taste of the utensils. Moreover, I had to get used to eating American food, such as salad instead of cooked vegetables, bread and potatoes instead of rice, iced water instead of hot tea, and dessert after every meal. The hardest part for me was eating cheese and butter. The smell of cheese and butter was nauseating to me. I lost seven pounds during my first week alone at Princeton! There I met many wonderful people who were instrumental in helping me improve my English skills. Roberto Baragan, of the admissions office, continued to assist me in getting free tutoring even though it was no longer his responsibility. My roommate Alvin Turner, who majored in English, helped me with every paper I wrote. I also took advantage of opportunities to interact with schoolmates from all over the country and overseas, practicing English and learning the American culture along the way.

When I failed the first set of tests, I was assigned tutors for practically every course. When they realized that I actually knew the material well but was too slow in writing down answers when taking the tests, my professors offered to let me take the examinations with tape recorders. After several months, my English had improved to the point that I no longer needed special assistance.

To earn some pocket money, I worked as a chapel watchman in the evenings, and worked in the stadium selling hotdogs and soda at ball games on weekends. These were very good jobs for me. The former allowed me to have a quiet place to study while getting paid, while the latter allowed me to watch football and baseball games free of charge. I finally understood why Americans were so enthusiastic about football and baseball!

At the end of the first semester, I became quite ill. While taking the biology final examination, I developed lower abdominal pain, fever, and nausea. At that moment I had to decide to either give up and take a make-up examination later, or just go ahead and complete the examination before going to the infirmary. I was so self-driven that I endured the pain, managed to complete my final examination, vomited right outside the classroom, and was then rushed to the campus infirmary. I was found to have appendicitis and had to be transferred to Princeton Medical Center where I was operated on immediately.

After surgery many classmates and professors came to visit me, including my biology professor. He said, "I knew you got sick while taking the exam. I was going to let you take a make-up exam when you recovered, but you don't have to now. You got an 'A' on the final (examination). It's amazing, you were sick while taking the examination, and yet you still got an 'A'! Whatever you do in the future, you will do well." I thanked him for his encouragement. When I received my report card, I found that I had received A's in all subjects except English, in which I received a C+. I was very thankful for God's protection and guidance.

One aspect of American life I did not care for was the casual manner of sexual relationships. Princeton, which became coeducational in 1970, was predominantly male in the early 1970s. Each Saturday busloads of women students from as far away as Vassar College in upstate New York were "imported" to campus to have fun for the weekend. Alcohol and sex were easily accessible on campus. After awhile, I withdrew from party scenes. Instead, I asked my supervisor to change my shifts to watching the chapel on Saturdays while others indulged themselves in wild parties.

Fortunately, I did not have to isolate myself socially. I was able to find a group of Chinese graduate students who were also Christians. Together we founded the Princeton Chinese Bible Study Fellowship. Every Friday evening we had singing, sharing, Bible study, and fellowship together. We enjoyed our time together so much that we sometimes would stay around until past midnight. The Fellowship continued to afford me spiritual support during my four years at Princeton. As most of the Chinese students came from Taiwan, I also learned to speak Mandarin (a Chinese dialect) through interacting with them.

CHINATOWN HEALTH CLINIC

"The Lord is my shepherd, I shall lack nothing" (Psalm 23:1).

After my freshman year, I got a summer job working at Beekman-Downtown Hospital near Wall Street in downtown Manhattan. My job was to study ways to improve services for Chinese patients. Each week I had the opportunity to work in a different department and to observe how the staff interacted with Chinese patients. I also interviewed Chinese patients in the hospital to gain an understanding of the language and other barriers to services. In addition, I visited various organizations in New York City's Chinatown. One of them was the Chinatown Health Clinic.

Chinatown Health Clinic was organized by a group of young college students who were concerned about the lack of accessible healthcare for Chinese immigrants. These immigrants were reluctant to seek healthcare because of financial and language problems. In response to this problem, the group raised money to start this clinic, which provided free medical care to Chinese immigrants.

The space was provided by a church rent free. All the laboratory equipment and medications were donated; all the staff and physicians were volunteers. I was impressed with everyone's enthusiasm and willingness to serve others so selflessly, even though many of them did not speak any Chinese. Starting in the summer of 1972, I joined them and became a volunteer there.

I helped by translating health education pamphlets into Chinese, setting up and managing the health mobile to do free health screening in the streets, and interpreting for Chinese patients. While working there, I learned to do many medical office and laboratory procedures, which I found very interesting.

One weekend I was assisting a doctor during a physical examination of a patient. I watched intently how the doctor listened to the patient's heart, lungs, and abdomen. Then timidly I asked the doctor what he was listening to during the examination with the stethoscope.

"What school do you go to?" he asked.

"I just finished my freshmen year at Princeton," I replied.

He acted surprised. Then he held up the stethoscope and said, "You need to go to medical school to learn this."

I persisted and asked him to let me use his stethoscope. With the patient's permission, I proceeded to listen to his heart.

"Why were there three heart sounds instead of two?" I wondered aloud.

Impressed with how I was able to pick up a heart murmur, he replied, "You really should go to medical school."

This was not the first time someone had encouraged me to go to medical school. As I mentioned earlier, my mother had wanted me to become a doctor ever since I was little. My high school biology teacher also had encouraged me to go into medicine because I always got 100 percent on every test in human anatomy and physiology. However, since I had not attended the British school system in Hong Kong, I did not think I would be able to pursue becoming a doctor.

However, after pondering what the doctor had said to me, it dawned on me that I was not in Hong Kong anymore. I was no longer restricted by Hong Kong's educational system that would have limited my opportunities. As a result, the idea of going to medical school was reignited in my heart.

MEETING MY LOVE

> *"He makes me lie down in green pastures, he leads me beside quiet waters" (Psalm 23:2).*

Chinatown Health Clinic did much more than influence my decision to pursue a career in medicine. It was also the place God had prepared for me to meet my wife, Jade, then the volunteer coordinator of the clinic. Her slim figure and the way she braided her hair reminded me of a schoolmate I used to befriend in the orphanage. Jade's attractiveness, however, went beyond her physical appearance. She was kind, considerate, generous, giving, and always put others' needs before her own.

For example, her generosity was evident at our group dinners. She was in the clinic almost all the time, frequently with no chance to eat dinner until after all the patients were taken care of, which was usually around 9:30 PM. Sometimes, after the clinic was closed, the volunteers would have dinner together. Jade routinely passed her plate around and offered everyone a taste of what she had ordered. By the time the plate was passed back to her, there was usually not much left for her.

I was also impressed with how much she cared about others, most of whom she did not know personally. In the summer of 1973 we organized a health fair in Chinatown. I was in charge of the nutrition booth, and she, the blood pressure screening booth. During the health fair, though, I ended up spending more time at her booth than at mine. For those with high blood pressure readings, she would patiently explain to them the potential problems associated with hypertension and make sure they had follow-up arrangements. Her personal care and touch was unlike anyone else.

Moreover, I found that she was very easy to talk to. After the successful completion of the health fair, the clinic had a picnic for all the volunteers at Bear Mountain State Park. We rode in the same car and had a good time joking around. Being with her was both comfortable and enjoyable. After lunch everyone had gone to swim, but I found her sitting alone on a rock by the beach. So I went up to her and started a conversation.

"How come you're not swimming?" I asked curiously.

"I don't know how to swim," she answered. Then she asked me, "How come you're not swimming?"

"I don't know how to swim either. I saw you sitting here all by yourself, so I thought I would come to keep you company."

She was admiring the blue sky and the perfectly tranquil water on the lake but did not say anything. After awhile, I tried to strike up a conversation again.

"Your English is excellent. Were you born in the States?" I asked.

"No. I came from Singapore seven years ago."

"How many brothers and sisters do you have?"

"This is not easy to answer. You see, I was adopted," she replied. "I am the only child in my adopted family. But I have many brothers and sisters in my birth parents' family."

I was so taken by her openness and trust in me with her

family background that I began to tell her my own story. We ended up spending the entire afternoon chatting. I was attracted to her, and I wanted to spend more time with her. For the rest of the summer, I helped out in the clinic quite regularly. After the clinic was closed, I would walk her home so that we could talk more.

As it turned out, we had shared similar adversities in life as children. First of all, she had been adopted at birth by her mother because her birth parents were too poor to take care of her. Her adopted family was not that much better off either. Her mother worked in a factory seven days a week. Her father was a sailor with the U.S. Merchant Marine and was seldom in Singapore. Jade and her mother later came to the States when she was thirteen to join her father. But, unfortunately, he passed away from stomach cancer only a few years later. My grandfather also had died from cancer three years after I came to the United States. Because we shared many similar past experiences, our conversation frequently grew deeper, allowing us to understand each other better and support each other emotionally.

She seemed almost perfect for me except that she was not a Christian. I knew scripturally that Christians and non-Christians should not be married (what the Bible described as being "yoked together"). So I invited her to church functions, hoping that one day she would become a Christian. Toward the end of summer, the church held a retreat at Paradise, Pennsylvania. At the retreat she accepted Jesus Christ as her personal Savior! It was then that I knew she was part of God's plan for my life.

After school started in September, we took turns visiting each other, spending the weekends either in New York or Princeton. Frequently, we spent hours at the bus terminal before reluctantly saying goodbye. After awhile, even the bus driver noticed us because he had to remind us several times that it was the last bus for the evening. I would then reluctantly board the bus. But as soon as I got back to Princeton, I would call her up and we would talk again, sometimes for several more hours. My phone bills were always over a hundred dollars each month, which was quite a lot of money for a college student in the early 1970s. At that time cell phones did not exist, and telephone companies charged for long-distance calls by the minutes. But it didn't matter to us. We were in love!

DILIGENCE REWARDED

> *"He restores my soul. He guides me in paths of righteousness for his name's sake" (Psalm 23:3).*

I continued to do well academically at Princeton and continued to pursue my interest in science with the intention of applying to medical school. My favorite subject was physical chemistry. Professor Naumann, a well-known scholar in plasma physics, included a bonus question worth thirty-five points on the final examination. I was surprised to learn that, in addition to scoring one hundred on my final examination, I was the only one in the class who could answer the bonus question correctly. So I scored one hundred thirty-five points for the final and got an A+ for the course. Later, Professor Naumann told me that among thousands of students he had taught in his teaching career, I was only the third student who had ever answered the bonus question correctly.

At Princeton, everyone had to declare a major in their junior year and start doing library and/or laboratory research for a thesis. In addition, a senior comprehensive examination was required before graduation. I declared my major in biochemistry and did research under Professor Marc Kirschner. My research was on microtubules, tiny structures inside every cell only visible by electron microscope. I worked really hard with the research team, sometimes laboring well into the early morning hours. After a year, and thousands of experiments later, we isolated an enzyme, which we named "tau factor," as the key to the process of how microtubules were formed. This discovery paved the way toward understanding several neurological diseases later on. After passing the senior comprehensive examination, I was awarded Cum Laude in biochemistry.

I applied to twelve medical schools. By God's grace, I was accepted by eleven of them, including Harvard, Yale, Johns Hopkins, Cornell, and Albert Einstein. The day before I received the letter of acceptance from Harvard Medical School, my premed advisor asked me, "If you could pick any medical school you wanted, to which medical school would you rather go?"

Without hesitation I replied, "Harvard!"

"Are you sure you want to go there?"

"Why? Harvard is number one in the country. Of course I want to go there."

"Well! I thought you may be happier going to a less competitive school."

"I'm sure I can handle it," I replied very confidently.

The next day I received a registered letter from Harvard offering me a place in the class of 1979 with a full scholarship. Praise the Lord! This scholarship was given by Princeton alumni who attended Harvard Medical School. The purpose was to encourage Princeton graduates to further their studies at Harvard.

I thought in wonder: *How could an orphan like me go from elementary through medical school with tuition completely paid for?* Even though I did not deserve it, He chose me first. He not only blessed me with everything I needed, but also "[threw] open the floodgates of heaven and [poured] out so much blessing that [I would] not have room enough for it" (Malachi 3:10).

I was so happy that day that I invited all my friends to join me for ice cream at a restaurant on Nassau Street. A week later, I cooked up a ten course meal and invited all of them to come. After the initial excitement was over, my thoughts turned to Jade. Since I would have to move to Boston to attend Harvard Medical School, and if Jade stayed in New York, we would be separated by quite a distance. How could we maintain such a long-distance relationship? We were obviously in love and were not willing to be separated for the next four years. Hence we decided to get married after my college graduation.

We talked separately to our respective mothers about our intentions. To our surprise, both objected! Jade's mother had become so dependent on Jade that she was afraid no one would care for her after we moved to Boston. My mother, on the other hand, was very superstitious. She thought that marrying an adopted person would bring bad luck to the family. Fortunately, Donna Chang, one of Jade's close friends, agreed to look after Jade's mother after we moved to Boston. I managed to convince my mother that as Christians we should not be bound by superstitions.

On August 10, 1975, we were married in uptown Manhattan's Presbyterian Church. More than three hundred fifty people came to our wedding. Fortunately, God again provided through our friends at Chinatown Health Clinic who all helped out by making dim sum and other refreshments for the reception. Otherwise we would have had trouble paying all the bills. However, we did manage to save up enough money during the summer to pay for a traditional Chinese banquet for our relatives following the reception.

After the wedding, we stayed at Manhattan Beach Hotel in Coney Island for two days before joining a bus tour to Nova Scotia. When we reached Fairfax, the capital of Nova Scotia, we were completely surprised to learn that the radio station there named August 15, 1975, Mr. and Mrs. Chun-Wai Chan's Day! Later we found out that it was the tour guide who told the radio station manager about our story, and they decided to honor us that way.

Upon returning to New York, we loaded all of our belongings into a U-Haul van. We moved to Boston, just in time for the start of medical school.

Chun-Wai Chan, MD

CHAPTER 5

LESSONS LEARNED AT HARVARD
(1975–1979)

IN THE GRIND

> *"The Lord is gracious and compassionate, slow to anger and rich in love"* (Psalm 145:8).

It was hard to believe that an orphan like me was able to study at Harvard Medical School. At Harvard I met many superb professors, quite a few of whom had won Nobel Prizes or other prestigious awards and had earned international recognition for their pioneer work in medicine. My classmates were equally impressive; most of them were top students from their respective universities. Moreover, because of the school's reputation, patients with all kinds of esoteric

73

diseases came from all over the world to be treated at Harvard. My scholarship at Harvard Medical School only covered tuition. The living expenses were my own responsibility. To save money, we gave up living in married student housing in Cambridge and, instead, rented a studio apartment at the edge of Roxbury just across the street from the Countway Medical Library. The neighborhood was not very safe, and the building was quite old. It took us a week to clean the apartment from floor to ceiling. We did not have enough money to furnish the apartment. But we needed at least some basic furnishings. So Jade cut up the cloth runner we had used during the wedding and made it into drapes. I built a daybed, a desktop, and a coffee table using scrap wood from a nearby lumberyard. By the time we were done "furnishing" the apartment, it was quite functional. More importantly, the apartment symbolized our motto: "There is nothing we cannot solve together!"

The first year curriculum at Harvard Medical School was very demanding. Every morning we had to go to the morgue to study anatomy with hands-on dissection. The autopsy room was cold and dingy. At the beginning, it was kind of scary. The stone cold corpse and the nauseating smell of the preservatives were almost impossible to get used to. The cadaver I was assigned to was a woman. I was not mentally prepared to see a person lying there whom I had to cut up a little bit at a time each day. It took me weeks before I was able to think dispassionately as I cut into this woman's every organ, muscles, blood vessels, and nerves, memorizing their relative positions so that I would not make mistakes doing actual surgery later on.

For the rest of each day, we had lecture after lecture in anatomy, physiology, pathology, pharmacology, and psychology, all combined according to the body's systems. The pace was rapid, studying one body system every two weeks and always ending with a final examination. The amount of reading material–about one hundred fifty to two hundred pages per day–was overwhelming. The method of study was also quite different from that of college, emphasizing memorizing facts over understanding the material.

Adding to the challenge was that I was enrolled in a combined MD-MPH (MD and Masters in Public Health degree) program, and I was determined to complete the studies in four instead of the usual five years. Also, many professors, though world-renowned in their areas of research, had such heavy accents I was unable to understand them half of the time. I was at a disadvantage because English was not my native tongue. I ended up spending a lot of time at Countway Medical Library, resorting to supplemental audio-visual material to help me understand the lectures. Moreover, I did not have money to buy textbooks, so I had to rely on the reserve library where all the textbooks and course materials were kept. Because I could not take the textbooks out of the library, I usually went back there after a light dinner and stayed until midnight, when it closed.

The heavy demands from academic pursuits caused a slip in my spiritual life and a strain on our marriage. I devoted practically every available minute to study, such that I did not go to church anymore. Jade, on the other hand, was bored being alone in the apartment. Each night she sat by the window, waiting for me to come home after midnight. After washing up, I often picked up my course material and studied some more instead of spending time with her. I could tell she was disappointed. But realizing that I had to study extra hard to keep up with the course load, she usually ended up going to bed by herself.

One night Jade suggested, "Why don't you study in bed next to me while I am sleeping?"

I didn't think it was a good idea, so I asked, "Wouldn't the light bother you?"

"No. I can still go to sleep with the light on. I want you to keep me warm," she replied. I felt bad that I had not spent much time with her, so I would take my textbook with me and sit next to her in bed. Invariably, though, by the time she would fall asleep, I also would fall asleep because I was so exhausted.

Somehow I endured many sleepless nights and made it through my first year at Harvard. In contrast, the second year curriculum was much more interesting. In the first semester we learned the disease processes, how they could affect the body, and how various systems were interrelated. The basic science knowledge acquired in the first year became much more clinically relevant.

In the second semester of my second year, we started to have direct patient contact. We learned how to obtain a detailed history and perform a thorough physical examination before deriving a list of possible diagnoses. We learned to follow clinical clues to make a diagnosis without the help of an ultrasound, CT scan, or MRI, none of which was readily available then.

Of all the medical instruments, I was most interested in the stethoscope. I would not forget what the doctor at the Chinatown Health Clinic had told me about learning this instrument in medical school. Besides using the stethoscope to take blood pressure readings, I learned to use the instrument for diagnosing malfunction of the heart valves, detecting blockages of the arteries of the neck and aneurysm (ballooning) of the abdominal aorta, assessing the severity of asthma, differentiating pneumonia from bronchitis, and determining if a distended belly was due to ileus (paralysis of the intestine) or intestinal obstruction. Most significantly, the stethoscope around my neck symbolized that I had entered the medical profession, albeit only as a medical student.

As for Jade, she was equally blessed. Several months after we moved to Boston, Jade got a job as a social worker at the New England Medical Center. This provided her a much-needed outlet to make new friends as well as a means to help with our incredibly tight budget. With her first paycheck, we bought a radio alarm clock. Each morning it served to remind me that Jade had been supporting me 100 percent and that I should never take her for granted.

With my direct patient contact, Jade became more and more interested in clinical medicine. I encouraged her to apply for the Physician Assistant Program at Northeastern University. Initially she hesitated, but after much encouragement she decided to go forward with it.

That program was designed to help Vietnam veterans who were medics in the military to transition back to civilian jobs. Somehow the program director made an exception for Jade and accepted her into the program with a full scholarship plus a $1,800 per year stipend for living expenses. We also learned that we would be eligible for food stamps if we moved to a more expensive apartment. So after our apartment had been broken into twice, we moved out of Roxbury and into the married student housing complex in Cambridge along the Charles River.

With both of us back in school, time went by quickly. We particularly enjoyed exchanging patient care experiences with each other, going over diagnostic workups and management of the patients we cared for, which reinforced each other's learning.

Jade and I also coauthored an article entitled "The Role of Chinese Medicine in New York City's Chinatown" based on the research we had done during the summer between my sophomore and junior years at Princeton. The article was published in the *American Journal of Chinese Medicine* in 1976.

At the end of my second year at Harvard, I received the CIBA award for achievement in community health, and the Rose Segal Prize for the best thesis on Community Health. I was presented the CIBA Collection of Medical Illustration and a $500 stipend. To celebrate, we spent the money on an unforgettable trip to Montreal and Quebec. For a poor medical student and his wife, this was a luxurious treat indeed!

I did very well in my third year of medical school, receiving excellent evaluations from my professors. During my internal medicine clerkship at Massachusetts General Hospital, the premier teaching hospital where everyone wanted to go for training, I actually saved a few lives.

One day I was talking to a patient. She suddenly stopped talking, her eyes rolled up, and her head dropped to her chest. I was the only person at the scene, and all I had was my stethoscope. I reached over, did a quick check, and found that she was not breathing and that her heart had stopped. I immediately yelled for help, laid her on the floor, and started doing mouth-to-mouth resuscitation. I was sweating all over, but I dared not stop. After what seemed like an eternity, but was probably no more than a minute or two, the resuscitation team finally arrived. As they took over, the patient woke up. The chief resident checked her out, turned around and said to me, "Good job, Chun-Wai. You saved her life."

Another evening I passed by a patient's room and heard a rumbling noise coming from inside. I went in and found the patient paralyzed on one side and unable to speak. I immediately notified the intern on duty. It turned out that his blood pressure had been extremely high and he was developing a stroke. We injected some medication in his vein to stabilize the blood pressure, and he started to improve. Within twenty-four hours, he regained all his neurological functions. At the end of the three-month internal medicine clerkship, I was given the award of "the person who saved the most lives."

During our clinical training, Jade and I managed to find time to take walks along the beautiful Charles River and the very busy Harvard Square, enjoying free sidewalk entertainment on weekends. We were enjoying our time together but at the expense of devotional time with God. After awhile we stopped going to church altogether. Without a church home and Christian brothers and sisters to be accountable to, it was inevitable that we started to drift away from God.

LEARNING IT THE HARD WAY

"A detached man pursues selfish ends; he defies all sound judgment" (Proverbs 18:1).

Consequently, when it was time to plan for my residency training, we did not ask God for guidance. Instead, I relied on advice from my professors who assured me that, with my academic achievement, I should have no problem getting into one of the Harvard teaching hospitals.

To get into a residency program, I had to participate in the National Resident Matching Program. Medical students would rank the hospitals where they wanted to go for residency training, and the hospitals would rank the medical students who came for interviews. A complex computer program would match the highest ranking of the medical students against the highest ranking of the hospitals to come up with a residency assignment for each medical student.

Four years of training at Harvard had given me a very good exposure to a wide variety of disease pathology and many diagnostic dilemmas. The breadth of medical knowledge I had gained had prepared me well to become a good diagnostician. Therefore, I decided to go into internal medicine. Following my professor's advice, I applied to all the Harvard teaching hospitals in Boston. But to ensure that I had a place for residency training, I also applied to teaching hospitals in Virginia, California, and Hawaii.

I went through a whirlwind tour of interviews at various hospitals across the country. When I was in San Francisco I heard that Kaiser Permanente Medical Center was also a good place to go for residency. So when I returned to Boston, I sat down with my advisor to see if I should also apply to Kaiser in San Francisco.

"What about Kaiser Foundation Hospital in San Francisco? Should I also try to get an interview there?" I asked curiously.

"Kaiser is an HMO (health maintenance organization). They see only healthy people. If you go there, you not only won't learn much from them but will also waste all the teaching you received from Harvard in the last four years," he commented. Then he added, "With your academic achievement, you shouldn't have to worry about not getting matched."

I was on cloud nine! With my professor giving me such a vote of confidence, why should I look elsewhere? Even if I was not accepted by the Internal Medicine Residency Training Program at Massachusetts General Hospital, at least I would be selected by one of the Harvard teaching hospitals. My ego began to take over. In fact, I was so confident of my acceptance by Harvard hospitals that I did not bother to rank any non-Harvard hospitals at which I had interviewed. Envisioning that I would probably be staying in Boston, we started to look for a home to purchase. There was a housing boom in Boston at that time. Housing prices were increasing each week. We went to open houses of new condominiums still under construction so that we could get a better deal. Finally we signed a contract on a brand-new, two-bedroom condominium in Cambridge within walking distance of Harvard Square. We also put a down payment on a set of contemporary bookcases from a furniture store at Harvard Square. I thought I had it made.

REJECTIONS

> *"Pride goes before destruction, a haughty spirit before a fall" (Proverbs 16:18).*

At the peak of my self-pride, I learned a very important lesson. On Match Day, I received a call from the dean's office telling me to report to her office instead of to the banquet hall. It was there that my classmates would receive their notifications as to which hospital they would go to for their residency training.

"Sit down, please. And please close the door behind you," she said invitingly.

I was very puzzled and asked, "Dean Eisenberg, is there any reason you called me to your office on Match Day?"

"I need to tell you that you did not match to any hospitals for your post-graduate residency training. I wanted you to come here to spare you any embarrassment you may have when your classmates ask you where you will be going for your residency training," she explained.

This was a huge blow to my ego and the most humiliating experience I have ever had in my life. I thought I was good. My professors thought I was good. My transcript reflected my academic achievements. How could I be rejected by all eight Harvard teaching hospitals?

Nevertheless, I thanked her for being so considerate. Then I continued, "I don't understand. My advisor told me that with my academic record I should have no problem getting into one of the Harvard teaching hospitals. That's why I did not bother to rank any non-Harvard teaching hospitals."

"Maybe you shouldn't have dropped all the non-Harvard teaching hospitals. What are you going to do now?" she asked.

"I don't know." I was totally lost.

"Don't worry! Residency matching is not the only way to get into post-graduate training. Why don't you give your advisor a call? He knows the director of the Medical Residency Training Program at Tufts-New England Medical Center very well. With Harvard Medical School behind you, I am sure they will take you in," she reassured me.

Sure enough, my advisor arranged for me to visit Tufts-New England Medical Center. The director of the Medical Residency Training Program there was very nice to me but did not offer me a position right then. When I did not hear from Tufts for two months, I finally realized that something was not right. The verse "pride goes before destruction, a haughty spirit before a fall" kept appearing in my mind. I was convinced that it was the Holy Spirit reminding me that pride had gotten in the way. With academic successes one after another, I began to think that I had made it by myself. God was no longer the center of our lives. Instead of trusting the Holy

Spirit for guidance, we were "leaning on our own understanding" for decision making. That's why God had to teach me a lesson by letting me fail in residency matching, which seemed impossible for a Harvard medical student with a good academic record and excellent recommendations.

Jade and I then got down on our knees and asked God for forgiveness. Immediately, God's mercy was evident. A heavy burden was lifted. The sense of worry and fear was replaced with a feeling of peace. Whatever happened, we knew God would take care of us.

SAVING GRACE

> *"If we confess our sins, he is faithful and just, and will forgive us our sins, and purify us from all unrighteousness"* (1 John 1:9).

How sweet it was to be able to come back to God and get reconnected with Him! Thinking back, it was so foolish of me to leave God who is infinitely wise and powerful, out of my decision-making process and rely on myself, who's so small and limited. Nevertheless, God's love for us had not changed. He used my failure to match to any residency training program, which seemed so impossible, to teach me to always rely on Him and not on myself.

I spent the next few days calling different residency training programs which I had looked into but had not applied to previously, to see if by any chance they had positions not yet filled. After the third call, Dr. John Witherspoon from Medical College of Virginia Hospitals responded. "We do have an opening. One of the prospective interns had a car accident the day after he received the notification, became a paraplegic, and will not be able to intern in our General Internal Medicine Residency Training Program. We have interviewed two candidates for the position but have not made an offer," he said.

"Oh! Really!" I was so excited.

"Is there any chance I can come for an interview for the position?" I asked.

"Actually, I was trained at Harvard also," he said. "When I saw your application from the matching program, I really wanted you to come to our hospital for residency, and I wanted to personally meet you when you came for the interview. But to tell you the truth, I was a little disappointed when you withdrew your application."

I explained to Dr. Witherspoon exactly what had happened. The next day, I flew to Richmond, Virginia, for the interview. The interview took all day, but it went very well. Dr. Witherspoon took me to dinner and then drove me to the airport. None of my classmates received this kind of royal treatment during their interviews for residency.

I took a red-eye flight home. When Jade met me at the airport, she was beaming and said, "Dr. Witherspoon called last evening. They decided to offer you the training position. He wants you to call him today."

God is indeed gracious and compassionate, slow to anger and rich in love! When I had not matched to any residency training program, I was totally lost and did not know what to do. The very next day, much before I had confessed and asked for forgiveness, God had already prepared a way out for me. Yet He had His timing and method. He wanted me to go through a winding path first, in order to learn not to trust myself and others, but to trust Him only. This reminded me of a song I always loved to sing, entitled "God Will Make a Way," by Don Moen. I could almost hear those lyrics as I fell asleep that night.

Since we had to leave Boston, we had to cancel the purchase of the condominium and the set of bookcases. Initially we were disappointed when the builder refused to refund us our deposits. It was more than a coincidence when one day Kathy Maloney, the department secretary from the New England Medical Center where Jade had worked as a social worker, called on us to say goodbye. During the conversation, we casually mentioned the dilemma we were facing with regard to our deposits.

"I may be able to help you," she said.

"Really?" We were surprised.

"Well, while I was working as a hospital clerk, I was studying part time in law school. I am now a lawyer working for a law firm in Boston. I can write a letter to the builder on your behalf. I don't think he would take advantage of you anymore," she explained.

We were so thankful for the perfect timing of Kathy's visit, as if someone had told her that we needed help. One week after Kathy wrote to the construction company, we received a registered letter from the builder. Enclosed with the letter was a check for our full refund!

The furniture store was a different story. The manager was adamant that the deposit could not be refunded but offered to ship the set of bookcases to Richmond. Since it became an interstate transaction, there would be no sales tax. He recalculated the cost. The shipping cost was, surprisingly, less than the sales tax. The total cost, due upon delivery, was actually less than the original invoice! We just marveled at God's intervention; His wisdom and timing were far beyond our comprehension. We finally understood why we should not focus on our own plans and that surrendering to God was the only way to fulfill God's purpose for our lives.

Right after the medical school's graduation ceremony, we went on a two-week trip to Hong Kong and Singapore. It had been ten years since I had left Hong Kong, and eighteen years since Jade had left Singapore. We had a chance to visit the places where we had grown up. As we looked at the rundown neighborhoods of our childhood, many scenes of childhood memories flooded our thoughts. We recalled times when we were struggling just to survive, sad moments over the loss of loved ones, and times we had been lost and didn't know what to do. At the same time, we were even more aware that God's hand had always been there and had never left us. Before we knew of Him, He was already working in us and for us. Through trials and tribulations He had shaped and molded us to become strong and courageous, so that we would be ready to do His work.

Upon returning to the States, we quickly made a trip to Richmond to find an apartment. We sold our old furniture, packed our belongings into a station wagon I had borrowed from my brother, and drove down to Richmond. It took us two full days instead of the usual ten hours to get to Richmond due to the Middle East oil crisis. We were allowed only three dollars worth of gasoline with each fill. We wasted much time waiting in line for gasoline and were exhausted by the time we arrived in Richmond that evening. The following morning I had to start a week long orientation before beginning residency training.

CHAPTER 6

RENEWAL IN VIRGINIA
(1979–1986)

SOUTHERN LIVING

> *"And the God of all grace, who called you to his*
> *eternal glory in Christ, after you have suffered a*
> *little while, will himself restore you and make*
> *you strong, firm and steadfast" (1 Peter 5:10).*

I n the 1970s Richmond was still very much a southern city. We found that people were cordial to each other, but relationships between ethnic groups remained superficial at best. We had several unpleasant encounters when trying to purchase large-ticket items. First, we went to a Honda dealership to buy a new car. No salesman would come to us to offer assistance. We finally walked up to a young salesman and asked for help.

"What do you do for a living?" he asked coldly.

"I am a doctor," I replied.

Immediately he became much more friendly. But with hesitancy he asked, "Did you graduate from a foreign medical school?"

"No. I graduated from Harvard Medical School," I responded.

Then he turned to Jade and said, "You've got it made."

Jade was so upset with his attitude that we walked out of the dealership without taking a car for a test drive.

Similar occurrences happened in furniture and appliance stores. In general, salespeople were hesitant to help us initially but completely changed their attitudes after learning that I was a physician.

We also visited several American churches. Again, people were polite but distant. When they repeatedly asked us our names and where we came from week after week, we started to question their sincerity in accepting us as part of the family of Christ. We did not feel we belonged to the churches we visited, though we attended their worship services each Sunday.

Meanwhile, I was completely consumed by the residency training program which was vigorous and physically demanding. Medical College of Virginia Hospitals had three main hospital buildings: one for private-pay patients, one for the publicly-assisted, indigent patients, and one for the incarcerated—the medical jail. The private-pay patients were cared for by the attending physicians. But the indigent patients and the incarcerated were the responsibilities of the medical teams. Each team consisted of two first-year medical residents and one second-year medical resident. Under the supervision of a second-year medical resident, the first-year medical residents became the primary caregivers to all patients assigned to their teams. The number of patients per team varied from day to day but was usually around twenty to thirty patients.

I was on-call every other day for a year, working thirty-six hours straight and resting only twelve hours before the next thirty-six-hour grind again. A typical routine would be the following: drawing patients' blood at 5:00 AM, examining all my patients, reviewing their test results, documenting their progress and presenting their cases to the attending physicians by 9:00 AM, participating in clinical conferences at noon, carrying out each patient's diagnostic and management plan in the afternoon, admitting new patients in the evening, answering calls from the nurses, and handling emergencies throughout the night. The next day I would repeat the same routine. Every other day I was able to go home around 5:00 PM. Most of the time I could hardly keep my eyes open while driving home. I learned to drive with one or the other eye closed alternately every few minutes so that my eyes could get some rest.

While I was busy doing my residency, Jade was again miserable at home alone. Dr. Witherspoon was our angel indeed. After he realized Jade's situation, he created a physician's assistant position for her in the Faculty Practice Clinic. The pay was not much, but it was a good way to keep her clinical skills current. Mrs. Witherspoon was equally kind to her. Every chance she had she would take Jade around town and introduce her to as many Chinese people as possible.

One day Mrs. Witherspoon took Jade to a Chinese gift shop and introduced her to the owner. Through her, Jade learned that there was a Chinese Christian Fellowship that met on Friday evenings. We then realized that in order for us to get settled in a new city, we had to find a church home.

The following Friday we drove across town in pouring rain, detouring multiple times due to local flooding, to get to the fellowship. Upon arriving, the brothers and sisters in the Fellowship welcomed us with open arms. Immediately we bonded with them. We were so thankful that we had finally found a group of brothers and sisters with whom we could have fellowship. With mutual support and encouragement within the body of Christ, we no longer felt lonely in Richmond.

AN UNEXPECTED REUNION

> *"And we know that in all things God works for the good of those who love him, who have been called according to His purpose" (Romans 8:28).*

Later on we felt led by the Holy Spirit to start a Chinese church ourselves in Richmond. As we shared the idea with the brothers and sisters in the Fellowship, we learned that another group of Chinese Christians was meeting on Sundays twice a month at Tabernacle Baptist Church. However, we were advised not to join them because someone told us that one of the lay leaders there did not set a good example spiritually.

We struggled for quite a while trying to decide whether or not we should visit the Chinese Christian Fellowship at Tabernacle Baptist Church. After much prayer and consideration, we decided to go and see for ourselves if God intended for us to become a part of this group. So one Sunday morning, after being on-call the night before, we went to the Chinese Christian Fellowship at Tabernacle Baptist Church.

The fellowship was a rather small gathering with no more

than fifteen people in attendance. When we arrived, the service had already begun, so we sat at the back of the room. I spent a moment praying silently to prepare myself for the worship service. When I looked up, the speaker had just gotten onto the podium. He was a former missionary to China. I was quite impressed with his preaching in near-perfect Cantonese. I kept wondering how he had learned to speak Cantonese so well.

Then I saw on the bulletin, which was written in Chinese, that his name was Rev. Mills. The orphanage I had grown up in had been founded by someone by that name. Initially I was so excited! The person who had meant so much to me was right there in front of my eyes! But at the same time, I was not sure he was the same Rev. Mills I had known in Hong Kong because he looked a lot heavier. It had been twenty years since I had last seen Rev. Mills in Hong Kong. Could twenty years have made such a big difference in a person? I wondered. For the rest of the service, I kept looking at him, trying to find any clue to decide if I had known him from before.

At the end of the service, I decided to go up to him and ask boldly, "Are you the Rev. Mills who was in Hong Kong ?"

With a twinkle in his eyes, he replied, "There's a good possibility I was, but it all depends on who's asking."

"I am one of your boys from Faith-Love," I told him.

When he realized that I was from Faith-Love Home, he hugged me so tightly I could hardly breathe, and tears of joy came streaming down both our faces. At that moment, I was convinced that God's plan was always the best plan. I had wanted to stay in Boston, but God had wanted me to come, instead, to Richmond, Virginia, for a good reason. I needed a spiritual mentor to help me grow closer to God. Therefore, God brought me to Richmond, Virginia, so that Rev. Mills could be my spiritual mentor.

From the time we were reacquainted he became a father figure to us. We enjoyed many meals together, reminiscing and catching up on what had happened in our lives. Our favorite gatherings were Sundays after church when he would invite some students to his home for lunch. He would spend hours telling us stories of his life, usually well into the evening.

He was quite generous with his love and fatherly advice. He helped us make many decisions, including formally establishing the Chinese Baptist Church of Richmond. Furthermore, he loved us like we were his own children. When our first daughter, Jamie, was born, he and Mrs. Mills waited patiently for hours in the waiting room, just like grandparents would have done. When Mrs. Mills saw Jamie, she took out a tape and measured her height and head circumference. The next day they came back and surprised us with a new outfit for Jamie, knitted by Mrs. Mills the night before. We gave Jamie the middle name Alma, after Mrs. Mills.

FINDING MY SPONSOR

> *"Ask and it will be given to you; seek and you will find; knock and the door will be opened to you"*
> *(Matthew 7:7).*

Since God reunited me with Rev. Mills, I reasoned that one day God would help me find my sponsor, Doris Hawkins. Without her, I would not have become who I am today. Although she did not know me, she willingly had sent five dollars each month to support me, providing me not only food and shelter but also an education and, most importantly, a chance to know God. Through her unconditional love I had come to understand the sacrificial love of Christ Jesus, giving so freely to us even though we did not deserve it. Therefore, I wanted to meet her in person, to express my utmost gratitude for her generosity during my orphanage days. However, I just didn't know when and how I would ever find her. I just prayed that wherever she was, God would bless her and keep her.

Lying awake one night in the hospital's on-call room, somehow the image of a postcard with a beautiful lakeshore kept surfacing in my mind. The postcard even had a post office stamp with "Muskegon, Michigan" printed on it. At first I was puzzled. Then I remembered vividly that it was the postcard my sponsor had sent me years ago. At that moment I realized that it was God who had brought this image to my mind, to help me find my sponsor.

With much excitement, I jumped out of bed and called directory assistance in Muskegon, only to find there were twenty-six people there by that name. The operator was nice enough to give me three phone numbers at a time. But after multiple attempts, I had no luck finding her. I had not given up hope, though. I knew, in God's timing, I would find her one day.

Then one night, out of the blue, I remembered that she was a nurse. So I called directory assistance to get the phone numbers of all the hospitals in Muskegon. I then called the hospitals one by one. Invariably the telephone operators of the hospitals said that they did not know such a person and could not help me. With each negative response, I began to lose hope. But I did not give up. I systematically called one hospital at a time each night I was on-call.

Finally my patience paid off. When I called the very last phone number on the list, the telephone operator of this hospital listened patiently to my story. Then she said, "I don't know your sponsor, but I can connect you to the night supervisor to see if by any chance she may know your sponsor." For a moment I thought that was strange. No other hospital operator I called had offered to do that for me.

I waited intently as she transferred my call. The phone kept ringing. After what seemed like an eternity, someone picked up the phone. It was the night supervisor indeed! I then explained to her that I had grown up in an orphanage in Hong Kong, and someone I didn't even know had supported me through the years. I just wanted to find my sponsor so that I could thank her in person.

"I know your sponsor!" she said after listening to me patiently.

"Really?" I was overcome with tears of joy.

"Ms. Hawkins was my instructor when I was in nursing school. The reason you could not get in touch with her through the telephone operator was because she retired and moved out of Muskegon several years ago," she explained.

After I collected myself, I asked her, "May I have her phone number?"

"I cannot give you her number right now. After all, this is very late at night. Why don't you give me your phone number? First thing in the morning, I will give her a call. If she knows you, I am sure she will call you," she offered.

God was indeed faithful. He had answered my prayer in His timing! The next day my sponsor called. The first question she asked was, "Are you really Chun-Wai, my Chinese boy?" I was so overwhelmed with emotion that I was speechless, but inside I was excited, happy, and thankful.

From the conversation I could tell she was a very loving and kind person. She wanted to know everything that had happened to me after I had left the orphanage. So we talked on the phone for over an hour, filling in all the details on how I had immigrated to the United States and made my way through high school, Princeton, and Harvard.

Soon thereafter, I took a week off and took my family to visit her in Pentwater, Michigan. The entire town came out to welcome us with a church gathering and a potluck dinner. We were deeply moved by their hospitality. Two years later, our second daughter, Janice, was born, and we gave her the middle name Doris, after Ms. Hawkins. We also invited Ms. Hawkins to Janice's baby dedication ceremony. Since it was the first time she had left Michigan, we took her sightseeing around the East Coast.

Thereafter we kept in touch until she developed Alzheimer's disease and had to be placed in a nursing home. Amazingly enough, each time I visited her in Michigan, her Alzheimer's disease would improve temporarily. Her memory would be restored, sometimes for as long as several weeks.

The reunion with Rev. Mills and Ms. Hawkins were two pivotal events in my life. In those situations I learned to listen to the voice of the Holy Spirit and not to trust my own understanding. Because I followed the guidance of the Holy Spirit, God rewarded me with the privilege of getting reacquainted with these two Godly individuals.

Even though I had grown up without my parents being able to express their love for me, God sent these two very special people to my life, and they became my surrogate parents. Their love for me more than made up for what I had lacked before. More importantly, their unconditional love motivated me to share Christ's love with others unconditionally.

Chun-Wai Chan, MD

SETTLING IN

> *"But seek first his kingdom and his righteousness,*
> *and all these things will be given to you as well"*
> *(Matthew 6:33).*

After completing my medical residency training at the Medical College of Virginia, I was asked to stay on as assistant clinical professor of medicine there. At Medical College of Virginia, they rarely, if ever, offered a professorship to someone right out of residency training. It might have been due to the fact that in addition to my doctoral degree in medicine, I also had a masters degree in public health with emphasis in epidemiology and healthcare administration. I started to give talks in these two areas. Soon I was a popular speaker not only for the medical school, but also for the school of nursing and the school of health administration.

As clinical professor in the residency training program, I enjoyed interacting with medical students and medical residents. They were all very smart, energetic, hardworking, and very teachable. Each day I made rounds with them, offering my advice on how to make diagnoses and how to manage patients with various clinical conditions. The questions they asked were very stimulating intellectually.

In addition to bedside teaching, I also gave lectures at clinical conferences. One of the more popular lectures I gave was on acupuncture. I had been trained in acupuncture during the beginning of my tenure at Medical College of Virginia, something very few medical doctors had done.

Administratively, I was given the responsibility of being the director of student health services of Virginia Commonwealth University. Originally, the student health services was an infirmary with twelve beds. The main function of the infirmary was to provide very basic, custodial care to students who were ill. If they did not recover in a day or two, their parents were required to take them home. It was a very inefficient operation.

With the support of Dr. Richard Wilson, vice-provost, the first thing I did was to eliminate all the beds and turn the infirmary into an outpatient clinic. If students required inpatient care, they would be admitted to the University Hospital, eliminating the need for parents to take students home when they were sick.

Within three years, I developed the student health service into a nationally accredited ambulatory care health service, providing clinical services, health promotion, and clinical research for both academic and health science campuses. The student health services greatly expanded to include the care of faculty and staff of the university community.

For research, which was required as a faculty member, I obtained a grant from the Metropolitan Foundation to study healthcare among college students. I wrote two clinical papers that were published in peer-reviewed medical journals during my four-year tenure there. "Health Risk Appraisal Modifies Cigarette Smoking Behavior Among College Students" was published in the *Journal of General Internal Medicine*. "To Screen or to Vaccinate? – A Decision Analysis of Rubella Prevention in a College Campus" was published in the *Journal of American College Health*.

As my professional career was blossoming, our Chinese church was also steadily growing. We started out with seven people, but within a few years the congregation had grown to over one hundred. By the time we called Pastor Kwok as our first full-time pastor, we already had a choir, a Bible study group, fellowship, and Sunday school for both adults and children. With Rev. Mills and other brothers and sisters at the church, we felt very comfortable settling in Richmond, Virginia.

TIME TO MOVE AGAIN

> *"Trust in the Lord with all your heart and lean not on your own understanding; in all your ways acknowledge him, and he will make your paths straight" (Proverbs 3:5-6).*

Before long, Rev. and Mrs. Mills expressed their desire to move to Fresno, California, following his retirement so that they could be close to their daughter, Muriel.

"The only hesitation we have about leaving Richmond is that we have to leave all our friends and start making new friends all over again," Rev. Mills told us.

By then we were very close to Rev. and Mrs. Mills. We really didn't want them to go. But we knew it would be better for their health to move to California. They would not have to deal with snow in the winter and hot and humid weather in the summer as we had in Richmond.

So Jade responded, "With your personality, you won't have any problem at all making new friends."

"Besides, if you move to Fresno, we will move there, too," I added. At that time we did not have the faintest idea where Fresno was. After the lesson we had learned in Boston, we knew we should not make a decision without praying about it. But we felt that if it was God's will for us to move to Fresno, California, He would provide us with three things: 1) a spiritual home there, 2) a suitable job, and 3) the sale of our house in Richmond, Virginia. We were confident that God would provide us more guidance, in His timing. After awhile, we even forgot about the matter.

It was more than a coincidence that at a medical conference in Washington, DC, in 1985, a nice gentleman sat next to me at lunch. After some casual conversation, I learned that he was from Fresno, California. I asked him all kinds of questions about Fresno. He was very curious as to why I was so interested in Fresno. So I told him the reason. Much to my surprise, he said, "We have been looking for someone to take my place as medical director of the health services at California State University, Fresno. Would you like to come for an interview?"

"Oh! What a coincidence! I would love to come," I said. I was dumbfounded.

The next thing I knew I was on a plane to Fresno for an interview. I was offered the job right away. Shortly after I returned to Richmond, however, I received an emergency call from our pastor's wife.

"Help! Pastor Kwok is not breathing." She was hysterical. Her voice was shaky and muffled by her sobbing.

I knew immediately that something was terribly wrong. So I called 911 for her, dropped everything in the clinic, and rushed to their home. I drove so fast that I arrived before the ambulance did. I ran to the bedroom. Pastor Kwok was lying in bed peacefully with his hands on his chest. I touched his body. It was stiff and cold. He must have died hours before in his sleep. This tragedy really taught us that the length of our lives is in God's hands. It had only been a week previously that he had undergone a rather complete health examination. All sixty blood tests had come back normal. No one would have predicted that he would be gone so soon. The only consolation was that he went to be with the Lord without any pain or suffering.

The following few days we were busy making arrangements for our pastor's funeral. After everything was over, Jade and I discussed our plans to move to California. We felt that until we found another pastor, it was not God's timing for us to leave Richmond. So I called the dean at California State University, Fresno, explained the situation, and apologized for not being able to take his offer at this time.

He said, "I understand. I can tell you are a very responsible person. Please give me a call when your church has a new pastor. If the position is still open, I will offer you the job again."

A year later, the church decided to call a pastor from Taiwan. I then called California State University, Fresno. I was disappointed to learn that the medical director position had just been filled. However, the following day, both Valley Medical Center and Veterans Administration Medical Center in Fresno called and invited me for interviews.

Right around the same time, we received a newsletter from Chinese For Christ New York Church indicating that our friend Jose Sy had moved to Fresno, California.

What a coincidence, I thought. So I called him up.

"Hi, Jose. I read from the newsletter that you have moved to Fresno, California," I said.

"Oh, yes! I am now professor of biochemistry at California State University, Fresno."

"How do you like it there?"

"I love it! The job is fine. People are very nice here. The church I am attending is a Chinese church. It is very small. But they have a very active college campus ministry."

"Is that so? Well, I have a job offer in Fresno, but I want to make sure we would have a good spiritual home there before making a decision."

"Our church needs more brothers and sisters. You should at least come to Fresno and see it for yourself."

After talking to Jose, I decided to go for the interviews at both hospitals. I went through the interviews and gave a lecture during their medical conference. Both places offered me jobs. I decided to accept the position of associate chief of staff for ambulatory care at the Veterans Administration (VA) Medical Center, with faculty appointment as associate clinical professor of medicine at the University of California San Francisco, Fresno program.

Prior to returning home, I visited the Fresno Chinese Gospel Church. They happened to have an evangelistic meeting that weekend. The speaker was Pastor Tang from Indonesia. Many college students accepted Christ as their personal Savior during the meeting. I was then convinced that Fresno would be a good place for us to be involved in God's work.

I also spent some time looking at houses. One of them was just right for our family, and I knew Jade would like it. So I made an offer and put a deposit down on the house.

But to move to California, we had to sell our house in Richmond. With the housing market in Richmond stagnant at that time, we were afraid that we would not be able to sell our house in a timely manner. However, we felt that if it was God's will for us to move, this would not be a problem. Amazingly, within three days of signing a contract with a real estate agent, we had three offers, each at or above the asking price! In the end our house was sold even before the advertisement came out in the Sunday newspaper!

With getting a job, finding a church, and now selling the house all happening so smoothly, we knew that it was God's plan for us to leave our comfort zone and go to a new place where He was preparing us to enter another chapter of our lives.

In June 1986 the movers came and loaded all our belongings and the two cars onto a huge cross-country moving truck. The following day we flew to California. At that time our daughter Jamie was four and our second daughter Janice just one. We actually moved to Fresno even before the Rev. and Mrs. Mills moved there. Despite many moments of nostalgia in relation to our friends in Richmond, Virginia, we have never regretted our move to California.

CHAPTER 7

SETTLING IN CALIFORNIA
(1986–1989)

TRANSITION TO FRESNO

*"Be strong and courageous. Do not be terrified;
do not be discouraged, for the Lord your God will
be with you wherever you go" (Joshua 1:9).*

The transition to Fresno was also amazingly smooth. First of all, the process of purchasing our new home took place without a hitch. With the help of Muriel Strum, Dr. Mills' daughter, and Terri Holland, a real estate agent, we did not have to go back to California for another visit. All the paperwork went through smoothly, including getting the mortgage. We closed escrow (finalized all the paperwork) on our new home in Fresno the day before we left

Richmond, Virginia.

We flew to San Francisco, rented a car, and drove to Fresno. It was pitch-dark as we drove through the mountainous area. The road twisted and turned, and it was difficult to see the way ahead in the dark. As I drove through the mountains, I prayed silently that God would protect us from an accident. Then it dawned on me that life was just like driving on a winding path. There were many twists and turns in life. When one encountered a bend in the road, one might not know what lay ahead. God had always been our guide. By just trusting Him we knew He would get us through. He always had and He always would.

We arrived safely in Fresno around 11:00 PM. The next day we went to our new home adjacent to the San Joaquin Country Club. While we were doing the walk-through, the moving van arrived with our furniture, our car, and all of our belongings. What precise timing!

We quickly unpacked the boxes, went to the supermarket, the gas station, the bank, and the post office. Within a week or two, we were settled into our new home. We also found an obstetrician for Jade because she was pregnant again. This was a pleasant surprise because Jade had made an appointment for a tubal ligation prior to the move. But when she missed her period, we cancelled the appointment. God gave us a son, and we named him Verent, after Rev. Mills.

Fresno has indeed been a great place for us. Fresno is located in central California, roughly halfway between San Francisco and Los Angeles. Surrounded by three national parks, the scenery is magnificent. The weather is hot and dry in the summer and rainy in the winter. Water from melting snow in the mountains seeps into the groundwater system of the valley. The climate is most suitable for growing all kinds of fruits and vegetables. Therefore, it has the reputation of being the fruit basket of California and the raisin capital of the world. Throughout the year, the freshest, sweetest, and cheapest fruits and vegetables are in abundant supply. After awhile we settled on a diet of mainly vegetables.

Other commendable features of Fresno include an outdoor orientation and an excellent school system. Both mountains and lakes are within an hour's drive from the city. Many outdoor activities, including mountain climbing, hiking, biking, camping, hunting, and various water sports, are readily available. Moreover, the educational system is one of the best, with the school district ranked sixth in the nation. The public schools emphasized the balance of scholastic, moral, athletic, and social development of the students. Many teachers were Christians. Our children received a first-rate education and excellent preparation for their futures.

MIRACLE AT FRESNO CHINESE GOSPEL CHURCH

> *"Consequently, you are no longer foreigners and aliens, but fellow citizens with God's people and members of God's household, built on the foundation of the apostles and prophets, with Christ Jesus himself as the chief cornerstone"* (Ephesians 2:19-20).

Fresno Chinese Gospel Church was started in 1973 by Rev. Moses Yu, originally as Chinese Student Fellowship at California State University, Fresno. At that time many Chinese students came from Hong Kong, Taiwan, and other parts of Southeast Asia. Many students became Christians while studying in Fresno. After graduation, most of them left Fresno for

bigger cities or returned to their homeland where job opportunities were more plentiful. Wherever they went, they continued to serve God. Therefore, Fresno Chinese Gospel
Church could be described as a place that trains and equips
Christian soldiers for God's kingdom.

We joined Fresno Chinese Gospel Church shortly after we
moved to Fresno. Even though it was a very small church, we
felt that God wanted us to serve Him there, and we grew spiritually in the process. We joined the choir, and within a
month, by default, I was the choir director. I also became the
Cantonese interpreter for our pastor during worship services,
since he spoke only Mandarin. By the end of the year, I was
called to serve on the board of deacons. The church was
blessed with a cohesive core group of brothers and sisters who
served selflessly. The church grew rather quickly. With the
guidance of Rev. Mills, we also rewrote the constitution and
bylaws to align the organizational structure and function of
the church.

The following year, we started a fundraising campaign to
build our own church building. Over $10,000 was raised in
1987, not a small amount for a church of only fifty or so members, most of them students. The momentum of the building
fund campaign continued for the following two years, reaching
about $90,000 by 1989. We started to look for an existing
church building to purchase. After our offers had fallen through
on three existing buildings, we decided to look for a site on
which to build instead. The population in Fresno at that time
was expanding to the northeastern part of the city. The area had
an excellent elementary school and high school. We figured a
lot of Chinese would move to this area in the near future. For
that reason we concentrated on locating properties for sale in
that area.

It was evident that God was at work in the process of land acquisition. On Memorial Day weekend 1990, most church members were away for a church-sponsored camping trip. Only Jade and I had stayed in town because I had to be on-call at the hospital. Our realty agent called to inform us that a 2.2 acre property was for sale, so Jade and I went to look at it. We figured that if it was God's will for us to build a church there, He would provide a way. Not wanting to lose the opportunity to acquire the property, I made an offer to buy it, contingent on the approval of the congregation.

"I don't think you should do that. I have never seen a buyer stipulate this kind of contingency. I don't think the seller will agree," our agent said.

After praying about it, we felt strongly that we could not make a decision for the church without the consensus of the congregation. So I told our agent to write up a purchase contract with the purchase price of $165,000, contingent on the approval of the congregation.

Surprisingly, the seller did not reject the contingency clause but insisted on the original price of $175,000. Two weeks later, at the general assembly meeting of the church, the congregation decided that we could only afford to pay $150,000. When I told the agent the decision of the congregation, she commented, "How could the seller agree on the selling price of $150,000 when he did not agree on $165,000 to begin with?"

"Don't worry. God will make a way," I replied.

Reluctantly, our agent submitted a counteroffer of $150,000. Much to everyone's surprise, when our agent presented our counteroffer, the seller, without hesitation, accepted it. The church saved $25,000. It was just incredible!

After purchasing the lot, another astonishing thing happened. The neighbor of the new property was apparently afraid that his house would be difficult to sell after a church was built next to it. He offered to exchange, at his own expense, the front half of his property where his house was situated with the back part of the church property. That way he could develop the land together with a new subdivision behind the two properties. With the land exchange, the church property went from a long rectangle to a square, doubling the frontage. This new configuration would make it so much easier for building design. Besides, without spending a penny, we had gained a house that could be modified to become classrooms and used for other purposes. Therefore, we agreed to the land exchange, and the process went quite smoothly.

What followed was a series of hurdles to clear in order to get the property rezoned for church use. The biggest obstacle was the master plan of the city, which called for a fifty-foot-wide street that would cut through the church property. How could we build a church if a street was to cut through the middle of our property? We worked many hours at City Hall to convince the city planning office to change the master plan. What complicated the matter further was that the councilman of the district where our church property was located was a non-believer. He was very much against any church being built within his district. The situation seemed to reach an impasse. The church-building plan was thus at a standstill for three years.

Fortunately, a Christian councilman became the mayor of Fresno in 1993. He understood our need, and he was instrumental in putting the church's rezoning proposal on the agenda at City Hall. In the meeting, he reminded the council members that churches are an integral part of any community. The City Council decided to call a public hearing to seek the opinion of nearby residents before making a decision. On the day of the hearing, not one resident came. The City Council went ahead with the meeting to decide on the proposal. When it came to the final vote, however, the votes were equally divided on approving and disapproving the proposal. The mayor cast the tie-breaking vote. The proposal for rezoning the property for church use was finally approved!

The church spent the next few years raising funds for the construction of the church building with a three-hundred-seat sanctuary. Many church members took out their savings and their retirement funds to donate or loan to the church interest-free. In December 1998, the main building was completed, with no debt incurred by the time of the grand opening. For a small congregation, this was truly the provision of God!

BRIEF APPOINTMENT AT VETERANS ADMINISTRATION MEDICAL CENTER

"Commit your way to the Lord; trust in him and he will do this: He will make your righteousness shine like the dawn, the justice of your cause like the noonday sun" (Psalm 37:5-6).

My position at the Veteran Administration (VA) Medical Center was associate chief of staff. Since the hospital was affiliated with the University of California, San Francisco School of Medicine, I also had a faculty appointment as associate professor of medicine. Each morning I made rounds with medical residents, teaching them how to diagnose and manage diseases in the field of internal medicine. In the afternoons, I attended to clinical functions of the ambulatory care division. Following that I spent time preparing for lectures and attending to administrative functions. The work there was considerably lighter than that of the Medical College of Virginia.

There was an evaluation unit in the ambulatory care division. It was basically the emergency room of the hospital, but due to regulatory reasons it could not be called the emergency room. Each morning veterans would line up in front of the registration area to be seen. At times they waited all day, only to find that at 4:30 PM sharp the staff, including the doctors, would leave, and they would have to come back the following day unless it was an emergency.

I found that to be unacceptable. I asked the doctors to stay until all the registered patients had been seen. In addition, I initiated many changes to make the operation more efficient. Some of my innovations included an appointment system to cut down waiting time and crowding at the outpatient area, a computerized medication list linked to the pharmacy to make it easier to match what medication patients were receiving versus taking, and renovation of the evaluation unit to improve traffic flow and bed capacity. The most significant accomplishment was instituting a hospital-wide quality assurance program to improve the quality of patient care and enhance patient safety.

The major drawbacks of working at the VA Medical Center were that things moved very slowly and that the staff was so firmly set in their way of doing things that it was difficult to motivate people to change. At times I wondered if the Lord wanted to teach me patience by bringing me there. On the other hand, I was thankful that they had a teachable spirit. Through building relationships, I was gradually able to influence them. A year later, I was making much progress. The changes were implemented, and both patient and staff satisfaction were much improved.

I could have continued on and enjoyed this very stable and still rewarding career with the federal government. After much prayer, I began to ask myself the question, "Is this what life is all about?" God had led me through a winding path. At this moment most of my struggles seemed to be over. I had a lovely family, a stable job, and a church I could call my spiritual home. I should have been content with what I had. But was that what life was all about? I kept on asking God this question. Yet for the time being, God did not give me a clear answer.

CARDIOLOGY FELLOWSHIP TRAINING

> *"Who, then, is the man that fears the Lord? He will instruct him in the way chosen for him. He will spend his days in prosperity, and his descendants will inherit the land" (Psalm 25: 12-13).*

One day I told Jade, "I want to quit my job at the VA."

"Are you serious?" Jade was totally unprepared.

"Yes." I replied.

"What happened at the hospital that makes you want to quit?" Jade was always so sensitive to my feelings.

"Nothing. This past year I collaborated with the chief of cardiology to conduct some clinical research. He really valued my expertise in biostatistics and epidemiology, and he appreciated my interest in clinical research in cardiology. Recently he told me that there's a vacancy in cardiology fellowship training. If I am interested, the position is mine. This training program is affiliated with the University of California, San Francisco School of Medicine, so it should be a high quality training program."

"Why go into cardiology fellowship training?"

"To take care of Rev. Mills! He has had several heart attacks already. If I become a cardiologist, I could take better care of him."

"OK. Since you have this intention, I support you."

So I resigned from the VA Medical Center and began a cardiology fellowship training. It was not an easy decision because Jamie was five and a half, Janice was two, Verent had just been born, and Jade was not working at that time. Going back to training was a huge salary reduction for me. We calculated what had to be cut back in order to make ends meet. But God was gracious. Somehow He provided all our needs and we did not lack anything during the two years I was in training.

During this period, though, the training was very intense, and the on-call schedule was extremely demanding. I had to be in the hospital by 8:00 AM and usually would not be able to go home until 8:00 or 9:00 PM. In addition, every third night I had to be available in case of cardiac emergencies beyond what the medical residents could handle.

During evening and night hours, I was the only one in the hospital responding to a variety of heart problems, including heart attacks, congestive heart failure, and cardiac arrest. After reviving the patient, I had to stay by the bedside and manually adjust intravenous medication until the patient was stabilized. Frequently there was no time to sleep. The following day would be another full day of work.

In addition to the busy clinical schedule, I had to conduct research in cardiology. Frequently I stayed at the hospital until very late to collect, tabulate, and analyze data. As a result, I had very little time left for my family. I was thankful that Jade was always so understanding and supportive of me.

Toward the end of my fellowship, I began to search for a position to begin my practice as a cardiologist. I could join a cardiology group practice or work for a Health Maintenance Organization (HMO). A Health Maintenance Organization (HMO) is a membership system. Members pay a monthly premium. If the member is sick and needs to see a doctor or go to the hospital, there is no or very little additional cost for care. About one-fifth of the population in the United States belongs to this type of healthcare delivery system. One of the features is that it combines the insurance company, hospital, and doctors' group into one. The conflicts of interest among the three entities are eliminated. The three entities cooperate with each other for the common good, resulting in much reduced administrative overhead and much more efficient delivery of care. In addition, an HMO emphasizes prevention. The healthier the members, the lower the cost of the operation, and for physicians, the lighter the workload.

When I compared the lives of cardiologists working in a fee-for-service with those working in an HMO, I was very surprised. I found that a number of cardiologists in town were divorced. Then I realized that the working hours of cardiologists were difficult to control. Heart attacks can happen anytime. Cardiologists have no choice but to respond to the calls and perform emergency procedures day or night. Therefore, it is difficult to set aside time with families. A busy cardiologist could make a lot of money, but at the risk of losing one's own family. Is it really worth it?

By then we knew that our relationship with God and with family should take priority over anything else. We decided that as a cardiologist, an HMO was the only option. So I studied different HMOs in California. Kaiser is the largest HMO and has the longest history of continuous operation. I felt it was my best choice. I actually started working at Kaiser as a part-time physician on Saturdays during the last six months of my cardiology fellowship training. As soon as I completed the training, I joined Kaiser and became their first cardiologist in Fresno on July 1, 1989.

CHAPTER 8

CAREER, FAMILY AND MINISTRY (1989–2002)

CAREER AT KAISER PERMANENTE

"But those who wait in the Lord will renew their strength. They will soar on wings like eagles; they will run and not grow weary, they will walk and not be faint" (Isaiah 40:31).

In terms of my professional career, I was truly blessed. As the first cardiologist at Kaiser, Fresno, I had the pleasure of designing the department according to my preference. Through networking with cardiologists from other Kaiser facilities, I was able to build the department from the ground up, including deciding on new equipment, recruiting new staff, and designing protocols for various clinical situations. Seeing the cardiology department become an integral part of the hospital gave me satisfaction and joy.

Most of my time was devoted to patient care. This included caring for both in- and outpatients; supervising and interpreting non-invasive cardiac testing such as treadmill, echo, Holter monitoring, and nuclear cardiology; and performing invasive cardiac procedures such as cardiac catheterization, angioplasty, and pacemaker implantation. The busy practice helped me become very good at what I was doing. For patients with heart attacks, I would use medication to stop the heart attack and then perform an angioplasty to open up the blockage and restore normal functioning of the heart. For patients whose hearts were too slow, I would implant pacemakers to restore the heartbeats. These emergency procedures had become second nature to me.

When a patient was dying, every precious minute counted. I would forget about everything else, become totally focused, and do my best to resuscitate until the patient was revived. When I finally saw the smile on the face of the patient and felt a sense of relief from the family, the incredible sense of joy and accomplishment I experienced was just priceless.

When patients and their families came to thank me, I would tell them, "Don't thank me. It's all God's doing. I'm just His instrument." Many times it would be a good opportunity to share the gospel. I then understood that God had His reason for me to leave my stable job as associate chief of staff at the VA and be trained to become a cardiologist.

After the cardiology department was functioning smoothly, I started to take on additional administrative responsibilities at the hospital. My first administrative assignment was to become part of the team that designed five new

Kaiser Hospitals in Northern California. In 1993, I became the chief of professional education. Within a year, I was able to build the program into a formal Continuing Medical Education program accredited by the California Medical Association.

When the new hospital was completed in 1995, I became the chairman of the professional practice committee of the hospital, overseeing nurse practitioners and physician's assistants. Six months later I was also asked to be the chief of quality assurance.

In 1996, due to the early retirement of our physician-in-chief (PIC) and the lack of a successor identified, Northern California Kaiser's CEO decided to select three physicians to fill the gap temporarily. I became one of the three assistant PICs to carry on the leadership of the Medical Center. So I steadily moved up the ladder to top leadership of the hospital within just a few years.

We divided the responsibilities into three areas: finance, service, and human resources. Since no one wanted to inherit the headache of managing people, I decided to take on the challenge and became the assistant physician-in-chief for human resources. At that time, Kaiser was facing tremendous competition from new HMOs that had sprung up everywhere in California. At one point, there were more than ten HMOs in Fresno. Many members left Kaiser to join other cheaper HMOs.

Faced with losing membership, regional headquarters decided to encourage senior physicians to retire early, and that their positions would not be filled. Instead, all remaining physicians would have to work four extra hours without pay. Many physicians were not happy with the mandate and left. Consequently, the workload of the remaining physicians became increasingly unbearable.

My first priority was to recruit new physicians to reduce the workload. At the same time, I expanded the continuing medical education program to teach practice efficiency. I started a reward and recognition program to enhance the physicians' sense of being valued. I also began various wellness programs to increase physicians' sense of community and well-being, as well as to help physicians attain a balanced life.

The effort really paid off. The downward spiral of physicians leaving Kaiser was stopped. New physicians were hired. Physician morale was significantly improved. Other Kaiser medical centers quickly followed our lead and began similar projects and programs.

In 2002, when the position of assistant physician-in-chief for risk was created to handle issues that could put the organization at risk financially or in reputation, I took on this additional responsibility. When the med-legal chief quit, I also became the med-legal chief for two and a half years until I trained someone else to take on that responsibility. In 2005, the hospital established an office of regulatory compliance to handle the increasingly strict healthcare laws and government regulations. I took on an active role in managing compliance as well.

As I wore many administrative hats in addition to my clinical duties as a cardiologist, time management became essential. I was thankful that the managers I worked with were all very intelligent and extremely capable. I did not have to do much of the administrative work myself. Increasingly, I found that taking on administrative responsibilities was essential in my mission to help others. In clinical practice, I helped my patients one at a time. In administration, by making the system work better, I extended my ability to help many patients at a time, as well as helping staff to have a better working environment.

Through direct patient contact and working together with staff over the years, I realized that life was not about me. The purpose of life was far greater than my personal achievement of fame and fortune or even happiness. Making a difference in someone's life gave meaning to my own life. The smiles on the faces of my patients, their families, and my staff validated the reason I became a doctor-administrator.

OVERCOMING ANGER

> *"No temptation has seized you except what is common to man. And God is faithful; he will not let you be tempted beyond what you can bear. But when you are tempted, he will also provide a way out so that you can stand up under it" (1 Corinthians 10:13).*

The busy schedule at work presented a challenge to my family life. Not infrequently, I was called by the emergency physicians or hospital medicine specialists for advice, even when I was not on-call. When I was on-call, awakening to phone calls in the middle of the night was routine. Occasionally I had to drive back to the hospital to perform emergency pacemaker implantation or cardiac catheterization and angioplasty on patients with life-threatening heart conditions. Time with my family was often compromised.

Sometimes I became short-tempered with the pressure at work. Very minor incidents, such as our children spilling milk, would trigger a strong outburst of anger. I always regretted it afterward. I hated it! Why did I have such a bad temper over such minor things? I knew it was not good for our family relationships. But I could not control my emotions, no matter how hard I tried. I just didn't understand it.

Just before I totally ruined my family relationships, God provided me a way out. In 1990, Dr. Peter Chiu, my high school teacher in Hong Kong who later became a counseling psychologist, founded the Chinese Family For Christ, Inc. Our family attended the organization's family vacation camp in Mission Springs near Santa Cruz every summer. We enjoyed the beautiful campground, which was in the middle of a pine forest, as well as the famous Santa Cruz beach nearby. More importantly, we got advice from speakers on how to improve our marriage relationship as well as on how to raise our children.

In 1993, the speaker for the family vacation camp was Dr. Wei-Jen Huang, professor of clinical psychology from Northwestern University School of Medicine. Very kindly, he allowed for one-on-one chats during leisure hours in the afternoon. Jade and I decided to take advantage of that offer so that we could ask for his advice on my anger problem. During the meeting we told him about our past and how I was so regretful each time I got angry.

He did not offer much advice, but he commented, "People who did not receive love when growing up sometimes have a problem with outbursts of anger." He added, "The deeper the wound, the longer the recovery." Acknowledging that it would take time to heal, he encouraged us to patiently wait on the Lord for His perfect timing.

That evening we watched a film as part of the evening program. It was about a little boy whose mother had passed away. His father, who worked far away from home, had no choice but to put the little boy in a boarding school. When the day came for the little boy to go to the boarding school, his father took him to the train station and helped him board the train. As the little boy's father stepped off the train, the little boy followed his father and refused to get back on the train. His father waited until the train was about to move and pushed the little boy onto the train just before the door was slammed shut. He then threw the luggage onto the train through the window. The little boy, while crying for his father, ran from one car to the next. The scene ended with the shadow of his father slowly disappearing on the horizon as the train pulled out of the station.

I could not stop sobbing, not because it was a sad scene, but because it reminded me so much of how my mother had put me on the bus to go back to the orphanage. Then I remembered what Dr. Huang had told us earlier. Maybe what he had said was right.

That night I told Jade that I had found the underlying reason for my emotional outbursts. I asked for her forgiveness. I also gathered our children together and asked them to forgive me as well. I felt as if a heavy burden had been lifted from me. What had happened in the past had been very unfortunate, but God had had a purpose in all that He had allowed to happen. I must not let the baggage of the past affect my future. Thereafter, I had more confidence in dealing with my anger problem directly.

Knowing the underlying reason for my anger was one thing. Being able to control my reactions was something else. What really helped me was the lesson on "The Family of Origin" during the family vacation camp. The lesson brought up the fact that childhood experiences can profoundly affect the life of an individual. Each time I felt upset I started to analyze my childhood experiences so that I could identify the underlying reason for my negative emotion.

For example, I used to be upset when my children scattered their things all over the living room, and when they didn't come to the dining table right away when Jade announced that it was time to eat. An otherwise enjoyable family dinner was ruined by me being upset. Then I remembered that at the orphanage we had to keep everything tidy and clean, and when the bell rang for meals, we had two minutes to stand at a preassigned spot in front of the dining hall. Those who arrived late were not allowed to eat.

How ridiculous it was for me to impose the same rules on my children and expect them to obey! So each time I was upset, I analyzed my childhood and frequently discovered the underlying reason for my anger. After I realized how my past experiences were affecting my emotional responses to certain emotional triggers, controlling my anger became a lot easier.

At times I had flashbacks of my childhood experiences, causing me to lose control. One day our son, Verent, was working on a model airplane on the floor of our living room. Our daughter Janice walked over, accidentally stepped on the model airplane, and broke it into pieces. When Verent cried, I immediately got angry and ordered Janice to stand in the corner, and Janice started to cry.

Then I realized I had made a horrible mistake. What I was visualizing in my mind was that incident in the orphanage, when the bully had taken the toy boat I had made from discarded popsicle sticks, stomped on it, broke it into pieces, and walked away. However, Janice had not done anything purposely to bully her brother. I should not have projected my anger at the boy who bullied me onto my daughter.

TURNING POINT

"What a wretched man I am! Who will rescue me
from this body of death? Thanks be to God—
through Jesus Christ our Lord" (Romans 7:24-25).

God actually touched me through our daughter, Jamie. During the summer of 1999, she got a job in a Christian bookstore. One day she was cleaning the stockroom of the store and came across a book entitled *The Other Side of Love* by Gary Chapman. She bought the book and brought it home.

"Dad, you may find this book helpful," she said as she handed me the book.

I took the book. The title somehow attracted my attention. Why had no one ever told me that anger was the other side of love? I hurried to finish my dinner and started to read it. I was fascinated by the author's logic about anger. He explained that since we are created in the image of God, anger is part of God's image. Since God could get angry, we were capable of getting angry as well. There was, however, a big difference between God's anger and ours in that God's anger was always justified, but most of the time ours was not. Then the book went on to explain the difference between justified and unjustified anger. The book cited many examples of unjustified anger, many of which I had committed in the past. Toward the end, the book offered many suggestions on how to restrain emotional responses to negative triggers.

Jade was a great help in this area. She had been praying for me. Then I found out that, through observation, she actually knew that I would be getting angry a lot earlier than I did myself. Therefore, we agreed on a method: whenever she knew that I was getting angry, she would not say a word but would bring a cup of water and put it next to me as a signal. With Jade's help, I began to notice that when I was about to get angry, my heart rate would increase and my face would be warm. Much like biofeedback, I gradually learned to sense these signals earlier and earlier. This provided me the necessary time to restrain my response to negative emotions. Since then I have not had another outburst of anger, and my relationship with my family has dramatically improved.

PART-TIME MINISTRIES

> *"I do not consider myself yet to have taken hold of it. But one thing I do: forgetting what is behind and straining toward what is ahead"* (Philippians 3:13).

With the problem of angry outbursts behind me, my interpersonal relationships with people outside the family also improved. Jade and I were able to become more and more involved with church activities and take on leadership roles in the church. At one time we were involved in many ministries. Gradually we learned to concentrate our ministries in two areas: child welfare and couples ministries.

CHILD WELFARE

First and foremost, I wanted to pay back the people who had helped me throughout my life, especially my sponsor. Because of her generosity and the generosity of the American people, I was able to have food, shelter, and the opportunity for an education at a critical moment when I needed help the most. The training and experience there shaped and molded me into who I am today. Most importantly, it was through my sponsor's unconditional love that I understood the amazing love of God. So I became a sponsor myself.

Over the years I have sponsored children through CCF (Christian Children's Fund) projects in Thailand, Indonesia, and India. From 1986 to 1994, I also served as a member of the board of directors for Christian Children's Fund, Inc., the very organization that supported the orphanage in which I grew up.

Just before I completed my two terms on the board of directors, I initiated fundraising for the Mills Endowment Fund to honor Dr. Mills' lifetime of service to humanity and to perpetuate his ideal of helping needy children become contributing members of society. In one fundraising trip to Hong Kong, over $30,000 was raised from among CCF alumni. The Chinese YMCA in Hong Kong also contributed $500,000 to the fund. That was enough money to get the endowment fund started in 1994. Over the years, investment income from this fund has helped many developing countries build infrastructure such as wells for drinking water, sanitation systems, medical clinics, schools, libraries, and career training centers. Countries that benefited from this fund included Mexico, Guatemala, Brazil, India, Sri Lanka, Ethiopia, Uganda, Kenya, Mozambique, and Senegal.

Furthermore, through word of mouth, I was able to get in touch with many CCF Hong Kong alumni who had immigrated to the United States. In some of the gatherings, many expressed interest to pull together financial resources to help needy children around the world, just like our sponsors had done. In July 2000, we started the Children's Garden Foundation and registered it as a tax-exempt charity without the help of a lawyer. Each year we raised enough funds to collectively support more than ten needy children in Central and South America through Christian Children's Fund.

After a few years, many schoolmates expressed the desire to help orphans in China. But Christian Children's Fund could not obtain the necessary Chinese government's approval to do business in China. So we started our affiliation with Sunbeam Foundation and Hong Kong Christian Council in Hong Kong, as well as Future Hope and Chinese Christian Herald Crusade in the United States. We currently sponsor over thirty orphans in orphanages operated by these organizations. We also have participated in helping over two hundred poverty-stricken children to return to school, as well as rebuilding a school damaged by earthquakes, to ensure that children have a safe place to study.

The sanitary conditions in remote villages in China were so poor that it was not uncommon to have both parents deceased in their thirties. Children left behind often become homeless, or they stay with relatives, frequently neglected, abused, or taken advantage of. One little girl was eight years old when both of her parents died. She stayed with her grandpa until he could no longer walk and had to be placed in a nursing home. This little girl had no choice but to live in the nursing home with him. Another case involved a family of four children aged five to eleven. Both parents had passed away from illness. Having no relatives to offer help, they stayed together in an abandoned straw hut. The eleven-year-old sister had to do odd jobs during the day and take care of her little brothers and sisters at night. Their food consisted of mainly porridge and a few pieces of vegetables. Their clothes were torn and filthy. In the winter they did not have any charcoal to keep their place warm. On hearing about their miserable conditions, how could we not be moved with compassion?

When these orphans were placed in the orphanages, their nutritional status improved and they became healthier. Also, given the opportunity, they frequently studied hard and excelled academically. One eight-year-old girl couldn't even speak Mandarin when she came to the orphanage. But after six months, not only could she speak fluent Mandarin, but she also was number one in English in her class. Quite a few children in the orphanages did extremely well in school. Several eventually went on to college. One of them wanted to be a doctor and go back to the village to serve the people there. It is really rewarding to see how they take advantage of the opportunities, study hard, and pave their way to a brighter future.

COUPLES MINISTRY

Having worked through the baggage from the past and learned how to control emotional outbursts, we felt that God could use our experiences for His glory. Even though neither Jade nor I were eloquent public speakers, we had the desire to be used by God. In 1996 we signed up to be trained as leader couples for Marriage Enrichment Retreats (MER). After training we were busy leading retreats in Northern California, first with Mandarin MERs. Later on, when the Cantonese MERs needed leader couples, we were leading both Mandarin and Cantonese retreats. Eventually, we also translated the curriculum into English and began leading retreats in English. Each time we had to drive several hours to the campsite. It was physically demanding. Sometimes we led as many as one retreat every other month. Fortunately, our brothers and sisters in church were gracious enough to support us by taking care of our children while we were away leading these MERs.

It was indeed our privilege to witness how the Holy Spirit worked in the retreats. In one weekend, couples who had varying degrees of marital issues were able to empty themselves and ask God to fill them with His love. With the enlightening of the Holy Spirit, they were able to humble themselves, put aside their self-centeredness, understand each other, appreciate each other, ask each other for forgiveness, and accept each other unconditionally. Many times we witnessed couples who wouldn't sit next to each other at the beginning walk out holding hands at the end of the retreat. We could not help but praise God for His awesome power of transformation!

We were amazed how God could use our successes and failures to help other couples. How I overcame my problem with anger and how we struggled to rebuild our relationship with our children were examples to which other couples could relate and from which they could learn. The most exciting thing was that some non-Christian couples, when immersed in the atmosphere of love and having tasted the grace of God, were often willing to open up their hearts and accept Jesus as their personal Savior. This was not our doing, but the Holy Spirit working in the hearts of these couples. Witnessing the dramatic changes in their lives confirmed for us that this ministry was very worthwhile indeed.

CHAPTER 9

TRIPLE HEALING
(2002–2005)

LOW WHITE BLOOD COUNT

> *"Praise the Lord, O my soul, and forget not all His benefits—who forgives all your sins and heals all your diseases, who redeems your life from the pit and crowns you with love and compassion, who satisfies your desires with good things so that your youth is renewed like the eagle's" (Psalm 103:2-5).*

I thoroughly enjoyed my career as a cardiologist and an administrator, as well as my involvement in various ministries. Before long I began to realize that I was increasingly busy. However, I reasoned, "I can do everything through Him who gives me strength" (Philippians 4:13). As long as the Lord gave me the opportunities to serve, I believed, He would give me enough strength to endure and the wisdom to prioritize and time-manage. Deep down, though, I did not know how to slow down. Jade even commented that I was like a car traveling one hundred miles per hour on the high-way. Sooner or later I was bound to have an accident.

Around mid-September 2002, I became ill while partici-pating in Kaiser's physician leadership training in Oakland, California. My white blood count mysteriously dropped to only eight hundred (with normal range being between five- and ten-thousand). Without natural immunity, I developed eleven painful ulcers in my mouth. My sores were so painful that I could not talk, had to numb my mouth with anesthetic, and had to blend everything into liquid before I could eat or drink anything.

With compromised natural immunity, I was at risk of con-tracting infections from patients. So I had to stay home. The irony was that as a physician-administrator and with all the diagnostic and treatment modalities at my fingertips, there was nothing I could do to identify the cause of my illness and to make myself better. I had never felt so helpless in my life!

One of the concerns was that this might be an early sign of leukemia. *What was going to happen if I developed leukemia? What if I developed the kind of leukemia that was incurable? What was going to happen to my family if I were gone?* All these ques-tions went through my mind. I was worried, distressed, and scared.

In desperation I cried out to God, "Lord, heal me so that I have more opportunity to serve You."

Miraculously, before I even finished with my prayer, a warm sensation went through my body from head to toe! Im-mediately the pain left me. The mouth ulcers were still there, but there was no pain. My weakness was gone as well.

"God just healed me! I can go back to the hospital now," I said to Jade.

Initially she thought that I was out of my mind. But when I told her what had happened, we both rejoiced and praised God for His mercy and love! I wore a mask and went back to the hospital for another blood count. That very day my white blood count began to rise. Within two weeks, it was back to normal. What an incredible experience I had with God's healing! It completely changed my outlook on life and my value system. From then on, I had to rearrange my priorities so that I could serve Him more fully.

One week later Peter Chiu, president of Chinese Family For Christ, called me and said, "For the past three weeks, my wife and I have been praying for you."

"Thank you so much for your prayers. God has healed me."

"I did not know you were sick!" he responded.

Then I learned that the day God had healed me was the same day he had started praying to God regarding asking me to serve on the board of directors in Chinese Family For Christ. Therefore, it was very clear to me that participating on the board was part of God's plan. Without hesitation I accepted his invitation to serve.

THREE HERNIATED DISCS

". . . I will restore you to health and heal your wounds,' declares the Lord . . ." (Jeremiah 30:17).

In order to devote more time to our ministries, I wanted to reduce my responsibilities at the hospital. At that time one of the cardiologists had retired, but we had not been able to find a replacement. So when I brought this request to my boss, he said, "We are already one cardiologist short. How can you reduce your hours?"

Patients need doctors. How could I ignore them? For that reason, I decided not to pursue this further until the cardiology department was fully staffed, so my busy schedule continued as before.

In March 2003, I was very busy one weekend while being on-call at the hospital. I had worked at the hospital all day and all night, doing all kinds of cardiac procedures. At midnight a patient passed out. His heart was too slow and required implantation of a pacemaker. In the middle of the procedure his heart suddenly stopped. I knew I had only about thirty seconds at the most before the patient would lapse into unconsciousness. At that moment every precious second counted.

With a surge of adrenaline, my heart was pounding, and I went into a resuscitation mode. To keep the heart going, I ordered the nurse to thump the chest of the patient every second while I worked on advancing and positioning the electrode inside the heart. It was by God's grace that I was able to place the electrode in a spot of the heart with ideal electrical conductivity, connect it to the pacemaker generator, and start pacing his heart, all within an unprecedented fifteen seconds!

As I was sewing up the pacemaker pocket, I suddenly felt a sharp pain at the base of my neck radiating to my right arm; my whole arm went numb, and I began to lose strength in the fingers of my left hand. I endured the pain, hurrying to finish the surgery. After asking my assistant to close the wound, I went home. The next two days I was completely bedridden because any movement of my head produced excruciating pain in my neck, as well as numbness and involuntary muscle twitching in my left arm. I knew this could be very serious.

On the third day I went to my neurology colleague who ordered an MRI, and I was diagnosed with three herniated discs in my neck, with one having actually ruptured. The neurologist referred me to the neurosurgeon. He saw me right away. After a detailed history and physical examination, he said, "You need to have surgery done as soon as possible. Otherwise, I'm afraid the numbness and weakness in your right arm will be irreversible."

"Can you give me three weeks?" I asked.

"What are you going to do in those three weeks?" he asked.

"I'm going to pray for God's healing," I said.

"Okay. But you will be back in three weeks and ask me to do the surgery," he commented.

Once again I experienced God's healing power. One day I looked up to see the birds on the roof of our house. I heard a "popping" sound in my neck. Immediately my pain was better, and I could move my head without causing neck pain! With physical therapy the numbness went away, and I gradually regained my strength. When I returned to the neurologist in three weeks, he was amazed that I had recovered without surgery. In my heart, I knew that God had healed me.

HEART ATTACK

> "Do not be anxious about anything, but in everything, by prayer and petition, with thanksgiving, present your requests to God. And the peace of God, which transcends all understanding, will guard your hearts and your minds in Christ Jesus" (Philippians 4:6-7).

The neck injury was another wake-up call for me to slow down. But with the cardiology department still not being fully staffed, I had to continue my usual busy work schedule. Eventually, after another flare-up of my neck problem two months later, the hospital had no choice but to allow me to slow down. I no longer performed surgeries or invasive cardiac procedures but continued to be on-duty in the hospital and see patients for consultations and follow-up in the clinic. I also started to train future physician leaders to gradually assume some of my administrative responsibilities.

In December 2005, while on hospital duty, I was paged to the critical care unit. A patient had a life-threatening tachycardia (rapid heart rate), and they were doing emergency resuscitation. As I rushed upstairs, I felt a dull pressure on my chest and a choking sensation in my throat. Arriving in the critical care unit, I was concentrating on saving the patient's life so much that I totally forgot my own symptoms. Half an hour later I was able to bring the patient back to life, and I had a chance to sit down.

As I was writing the report, I realized that during the entire time my chest pressure had not gone away. Initially I ignored it because, having no history of any cardiac risk factor such as smoking, hypertension, high cholesterol, being overweight, or having a family history of heart attack, I did not think I could have a heart attack. When the symptoms did not resolve in twenty minutes, I casually mentioned my situation to my colleague who happened to be sitting next to me at the work station in the critical care unit.

"I've never had this before, but I've had this chest pressure and choking sensation for almost an hour now. I'm wondering if I am having a heart attack," I said.

"Are you serious! You are a heart doctor," my colleague said. "You ought to know better!"

Immediately he rushed me to the emergency department. The EKG confirmed that I was having a heart attack right then. Praise be to God! He was merciful! With oxygen and a nitroglycerin patch, I was symptom-free within a few minutes. Subsequent blood tests did not show any damage of the heart muscles, but the abnormalities on the EKG persisted.

For the first time in my life, I realized that I could not take life for granted. I just had a heart attack, and I could have died. Every breath I took was indeed a blessing from God, the Creator and Sustainer of all things. At the same time, strangely enough, the song "It is Well With my Soul," kept echoing over and over again in my mind. While lying on the gurney in the emergency department I had a sense of peace that was very difficult to describe. I was certain that God was watching over me. Whatever happened, He was teaching me to say, "It is well with my soul."

The chief of the emergency department who was taking care of me came to my bedside. "Your EKG is very abnormal. I want to keep you in the hospital for observation and then do cardiac catheterization," she said.

"I can't do that," I replied. "Today is Friday. I am supposed to lead a Bible study in the fellowship group at our home. I need to go back home," I begged.

"Doctors are the worst patients. But if you insist, I cannot stop you." She was not pleased at all with my request. Nevertheless, she let me go, albeit reluctantly, after I promised to return to the emergency department immediately if symptoms recurred.

I cannot advocate that anyone should do the same. But God was at work and I was truly blessed. Throughout the weekend I was fine. On Monday morning I went to the hospital for the angiogram. Sure enough, there was an almost completely blocked area, followed by another significantly blocked area on the left coronary artery.

"Can you infuse some medication into the blocked artery to make sure that it was not a coronary spasm?" I asked my colleague who was doing the procedure.

"In my years of experience in cardiac catheterization, I have not seen focal blockages like that caused by a spasm. But since you insist, I will do it."

He infused some medication into the blocked artery, and nothing happened.

"See, this is not a coronary spasm. I think we need to go ahead with balloon angioplasty."

"Okay, go ahead," I replied.

I signed the consent form to authorize the team to go ahead with the procedure. One of the nurses went to the waiting room to inform Jade of the decision while my colleague took the catheter out of the artery in my arm, applied pressure to stop the bleeding, and put another catheter into the artery in my groin. The preparation took about forty minutes, during which time I lay quietly on the operating table and prayed for God to carry me through the angioplasty procedure.

God was indeed faithful. He did more than I had requested. He intervened by taking the lesions away, right before our eyes! When my colleague was ready to pass the wire down the blocked artery, he found that the blockages were completely gone. "With the thousands of procedures I have performed in my career, I have never seen this before," he remarked.

So he repeated the catheterization procedure to ensure it was not a mistake. Indeed, the arteries were as clean as a teenager's! He was puzzled, and then he reasoned, "The blockages identified earlier must be atypical, prolonged coronary spasm. There is no need for angioplasty anymore." But the nurse assisting the procedure commented, "Dr. Chan, I have been watching you. I saw that you were praying. You must have been praying really hard, weren't you?" "Praise the Lord. He heard my prayer. Actually, I was praying for the procedure to be smooth and without complications. God gave me more than I asked for. He removed the blockages and replaced them with brand-new coronary arteries," I replied.

It turned out that all this time Jade had also been praying in the waiting room for God to take the blockages away. God answered our prayers! I left the hospital that afternoon without balloon angioplasty, but with a renewed understanding that ". . . neither death nor life, neither angels nor demons, neither the present nor the future, nor any powers, neither height nor depth, nor anything else in all creation, will be able to separate us from the love of God that is in Christ Jesus our Lord" (Romans 8:38-39).

BE STILL

"Be still, and know that I am God; I will be exalted among the nations, I will be exalted in the earth"
(Psalm 46:10).

Looking back, God was telling me not once or twice, but three times, to slow down. Each warning was stronger than the previous one. But I had very good excuse not to. I needed to save lives. Each day patients were dying from heart attacks or other life-threatening heart conditions. It was my call-of-duty to help these people the best I knew how. How could I slow down?

"Be still, and know that I am God" (Psalm 46:10). This verse reminded me that when I was busy saving lives, the recurring sense of accomplishment from lives saved actually pulled me away from humility and meekness in Christ, and pushed me into self-centered confidence and pride. Subconsciously I was no longer seeking God's glory but my own. I was so thankful that God forced me to be still through illness. Only by being still would I have the luxury of solitude–to reflect and reassess the purpose, meaning, and priorities of my life.

Through this experience I learned two things: 1) health is one of the most important God-given treasures in life, for without it I could not do anything for the Lord; and 2) life is not about me. The purpose of life is far greater than my own personal accomplishment. When we finally meet God face to face, the only things that matter will be: our relationship with God, our relationship with our own family, and how we touched the lives of people with whom God entrusted us.

CHAPTER 10

LIFE INFLUENCING LIFE
(2005–PRESENT)

SERVICES AT KAISER

*"For we are God's workmanship, created in Christ
to do good works, which God prepared in advance
for us to do" (Ephesians 2:10).*

After my ordeal with my heart condition, the hospital was finally convinced that I really needed to slow down. So I was relieved of being on-call and working in the hospital. My clinical duty was limited to outpatient consultation and follow-up half-time. The other half of the time I spent in administrative duties. With the new schedule, I was no longer awakened in the middle of the night to take care of cardiac emergencies. My general health continued to improve. At first I was depressed about not being able to do cardiac procedures. Invasive and interventional procedures were extremely rewarding because the gratification was instant when a heart attack was stopped and the function of a heart restored. When I could no longer do the procedures, I felt part of my life was gone. Each time my patient needed a procedure, I had to ask my colleagues to do it on my behalf. I felt handicapped, de-valued, and inferior.

As I was pouring my heart out to the Lord, God spoke to me through the following Bible verse: "If anyone serves, he should do it with the strength God provides, so that in all things God may be praised through Jesus Christ" (1 Peter 4:11). I then realized that life is not up to us. In order to effectively deal with the many changes in life, I had to be more flexible. Besides, if God took away my ability to perform cardiac procedures, what area of strength would God provide me instead? How could I continue to serve Him and glorify Him? Once my servanthood attitude was realigned, I had a sense of renewal and rejuvenation.

Over time I found that I could serve my patients and colleagues most effectively by person-to-person encounters. Through my involvement with couple's ministry over the years, God had prepared for me a new niche in my professional career: dealing with difficult patients and handling conflicts between doctors and staff.

Dealing with difficult patients required good communication skills. Some patients were so critical and demanding that they changed doctors as many as fifteen times. Others were always suspicious of Kaiser trying to cut costs each time doctors did not order tests they wanted. Still others accused doctors of negligence when surgery or medical management resulted in complications or simply did not give the desired result.

I learned to establish rapport with them by finding commonalities and I expressed empathy by listening and showing understanding. Once the channel of communication opened up, I could then help them differentiate their needs from their wants and assist them in getting the services they needed, though not necessarily what they wanted. I routinely contacted them again to make sure they were satisfied with the care. The same communication skills have been useful in managing conflicts between doctors and staff. Doctors are smart and skillful, but their interpersonal relationships may not be as skilled. Some have problems handling stress and cannot control their emotions when working under pressure. Others have such high expectations of their staff that no one can live up to their standards. Still others cannot work as part of a team.

I learned to influence them, emphasizing that people might not remember what we have said or even what we have done, but they will never forget how we have made them feel. In addition, I tried to inspire them to be kind and merciful and to let no one come to them without going away feeling better.

Occasionally I had to mediate conflicts when the chiefs and managers could not handle them. Invariably I used biblical principles to counsel them. For example, verses such as "Everyone should be quick to listen, slow to speak and slow to become angry" (James 1:19), "Do nothing out of selfish ambition or vain conceit, but in humility consider others better than yourselves. Each of you should look not only to your own interests, but also to the interests of others" (Philippians

2:3-4), and "Be kind and compassionate to one another, forgiving each other, just as in Christ God forgave you" (Ephesians 4:32) were very useful. Even though many weren't Christians, quite a few were teachable. As long as I showed understanding and cared about them, they were quite receptive to the enlightenment of the truth. When they adjusted their attitudes, their interpersonal relationships improved. Then they could realize their full potential in working as a team and serving others.

Over the years my professional colleagues honored me with different awards and recognition. This included the Paul Harris Fellow award by Rotary Foundation of Rotary International, David Lawrence Community Service Award from the National Kaiser Foundation Health Plan (for international voluntarism), "Everyday Hero" award from Northern California Kaiser Region, the "Asian-American Heritage" award from Kaiser Permanente Asian Association, as well as the "Special Project Services" award from Fresno-Madera Medical Society. I was grateful for these awards. Nevertheless, I know very well that all the fame and fortune on earth mean nothing compared to meeting the Lord face-to-face in heaven.

MINISTRIES IN CHINA

> *"Commit to the Lord whatever you do, and your plans will succeed" (Proverbs 16:3).*

Beginning in 2007, I have had several opportunities to visit hospitals in China. This all started with executive directors of hospitals in China visiting our hospital to learn how we managed healthcare services. To reciprocate, they invited me to visit them as part of a cultural exchange program. Some of the hospitals were trying to improve their services to meet international standards. I thought it was a good idea because I could contribute to improving the quality of healthcare services in China through this program. At the same time, I could also visit the orphanages we had supported.

Jade and I had no idea why God had given us the opportunity to visit hospitals in China. But if God gave us the opportunity to lead just one person to Christ, it would then be worth the effort of making the trips. We prayed about it. We had peace with it. So we agreed to go.

Amazingly, God gave us several opportunities to witness to people there about Christ. During dinner with the senior staff of the hospital, someone out of the blue asked, "How do you know the Bible was inspired by God?" We took the opportunity to talk about the Bible, but hesitated to continue when they changed the subject.

One day, one of the senior staff and the hospital chauffeur took us to visit another city. As we were enjoying the beautiful scenery along the highway, Jade asked them, "Is there a church we can visit on Sunday?"

"I don't know, but we can find out."

"What do you think about churches?" Jade asked boldly.

"We don't believe in religion. We don't go to church. But it sounds like you two are Christians."

"Yes. Christianity is very important in our lives."

"What is the advantage of being a Christian?"

"There are many advantages: joy and peace on earth and eternal life in heaven, to name a few."

"No. We are Communist Party members. We cannot talk about religion," the chauffeur added.

We didn't dare to continue the conversation. So our brief moment of evangelism ended abruptly. But toward the end of our trip, one of the senior staff came to our hotel room and said to us privately, "I noticed something unusual about you two. You have a certain peace and contentment that most of us don't have. I would like to know more about your God."

His desire to seek the truth was just like Nicodemus in the Bible. So we immediately jumped at the chance to explain the gospel to him. We praised God for allowing us to serve Him in unusual circumstances. Even though he did not accept Jesus Christ as his personal Savior right away, the seed of the gospel had been sown. We got a Bible and a Christian book from a friend and gave it to him. He promised to read the book and the Bible daily.

After our trip, several senior staff from the hospital came to visit us in Fresno. This gave us an unrestricted opportunity to share the gospel with them. Two of them were particularly interested in hearing about Christ. Toward the end of their visit, they commented that they believed in God, but it was too difficult to make a commitment to become Christians because too much of their future would be at stake. We replied that they should take their time to study the Bible and not rush into a decision. A year later, both of them decided to become Christians! We praised God for His faithfulness. He let us witness to people we came in contact with in China. Two of them subsequently became Christians, which was more than we had asked for.

FAMILY RELATIONSHIP MINISTRIES

"And let us consider how we may spur one another on toward love and good deeds" (Hebrews 10:24).

In His marvelous way, God also prepared us to serve in a

slightly different couples ministry: family relationship ministry. Twelve years with Chinese Family For Christ had equipped us well to lead couples in retreats. Increasingly, though, we realized that a large percentage of blue collar couples and couples with young children could not take advantage of what the retreats had to offer because it was hard for them financially to get three days off and to be away from their children for that long. As our hearts were compelled to minister to these couples, we began to explore other ways to serve them, even though we knew from experience that the three-day retreat format was the most effective.

In time we got acquainted with Dr. Elmer Martens, president-emeritus of the Mennonite Brethren Biblical Seminary in Fresno. He encouraged us to go to seminary to study so that we would be better equipped to serve God. I tried to juggle my work schedule to fit the class schedule, but with my full-time job it was just too difficult.

One day, while preparing for a marriage workshop we were going to conduct in New York, we came across a website about marriage mentoring. We were surprised that the Fresno County Healthy Marriage Coalition had a branch called Marriage Mentoring Ministry right here in Fresno. That same evening I was speechless when I received an e-mail from Dr. Martens.

"Since it doesn't seem possible for you to take classes in the seminary, you should check into the possibility of getting involved with the Marriage Mentoring Ministries in Fresno," he wrote.

"This is more than coincidence. It has to be the guidance of the Holy Spirit," I told Jade. So we sent an e-mail to the founder, Mr. Ron McLain. He replied right away, saying, "We have been praying for God to open doors for the ministry to reach out to other ethnic communities. You are the first Asian couple to contact us. Praise God! He has answered our prayers!"

Within a week, Mr. and Mrs. McLain came to visit us at our home. We connected right away and talked for several hours, just like old friends. In the following few months we attended their mentoring training and the couple communication course entitled "Mastering the Mystery of Love." We also became facilitators. We have enjoyed teaching the seminars in various churches in Fresno. It was so gratifying to see couples with strained relationships holding hands and smiling at each other after taking the course, sometimes after just one session. To better equip myself, I also started to take seminary courses at Gordon-Conwell Theological Seminary through the Internet.

The experiences of leading seminars in Caucasian churches were great. However, our deepest desire was to help more Chinese couples. Owing to cultural influences, which tend to suppress open expression of feelings and needs, many Chinese couples face unique issues in their marital relationships. Yet once they have gotten beyond the cultural influences and have learned to communicate openly, the improvement in their marital relationships were often dramatic.

With encouragement from Mr. McLain, we translated the mentoring training curriculum as well as the communication course into Chinese, with some revisions tailored to Chinese couples' cultural background and social situation. Since 2008, we have been introducing the mentoring and couple communication courses in Chinese churches in Fresno. As time went on, we found that other people such as single parents and the unmarried could benefit from the same communication training. Therefore, our training expanded to include singles and college students.

We are equally thankful that the Lord has opened many doors for us to bring family relationship seminars to Chinese churches in Northern, Central, and Southern California, Utah, Ohio, New Jersey, and New York. Consequently, we spend many weekends and most of our vacation time traveling to various places to lead these seminars. The joy we experience in serving Him through this ministry more than compensates for the physical fatigue we have after a lengthy trip.

Besides leading seminars, we are especially thankful for the opportunity to help couples one-on-one. Some of them live far away from us. But we manage to mentor them through telephone or Internet webcam. Couples' issues vary, ranging from not talking to each other to yelling, screaming, and physically fighting with one another. Other issues include difficulty communicating with teenage children and conflicts between pastors and lay leaders in the church.

We are not licensed counselors. We are completely relying on the Holy Spirit to guide us as we listen to their complaints, show understanding of their situations, and walk with them for a short while in their journey of life. The most important thing we can do is to use God's Word to enlighten them, help them turn to God so that they can crucify their old selves, be kind and merciful to each other, forgive each other, accept each other, and rebuild their relationships.

Some couples change completely after a few sessions. Others struggle for a long time without any sign of improvement. Sometimes we have had to take a break. But amazingly, when we are just about to give up, relationships improve without our help. This illustrates that it is all God's grace and mercy working through the Holy Spirit. In God's timing they turn around. And however it happens, we are so happy to see the transformation. We believe the angels in heaven also rejoice. Seeing lives changed helps reaffirm our commitment to this ministry. We firmly believe that the Lord has His plan for us. As long as He gives us the strength and opens doors, we will continue to serve Him in this ministry.

LOOKING FORWARD

> *"Remember not the sins of my youth and my re-bellious ways; according to your love remember me, for you are good, O Lord"* (Psalm 25:7).

Thinking about how much time I have left in this world can be depressing. True, life is not up to us, just as the Scripture says, "Why, you do not even know what will happen tomorrow. What is your life? You are a mist that appears for a little while and then vanishes" (James 4:14). With life being so unpredictable, I sometimes wondered how I could make the best of my remaining years. For all the mistakes I have made in the past, besides confessing to God and asking for His mercy, how could I move forward?

When I look at my past and look forward to the future, I have a sense of peace and contentment because I have found answers to many of my questions about life. God chose me to be His child even before I was born. He put me in a poor family at birth in order to train me to persevere. He let me fall at the height of my academic success in order to teach me to remain humble and meek. He used illness at the peak of my professional career to make me reevaluate my servant attitude and direction. God has never left me or forsaken me. He has always been there by my side. All the adversity and failure were lessons taught by God, to train me to become a faithful servant of His, and to mold me into a useful vessel.

From my experiences of serving in various ministries, I have discovered that I can serve God more effectively in this world, not with a huge program requiring large sums of money and resources, but by slowly and quietly making an impact in someone's life, one life at a time. This is how I would leave my legacy for future generations.

When we recognize our own mortality and vulnerability, our lives carry new meaning. The journey of life on earth is like taking a train, passing through one station after another until one reaches the final stop. But it is not the final destination. For those who are saved by grace, a shuttle bus is waiting at the station, taking the believers to heaven. There we have the everlasting presence of God and eternal joy. Therefore, life is no longer just about temporal success but about serving God by making a difference in the lives of others. When I meet God face to face, I hope God will say, "Well done, good and faithful servant! You have been faithful with a few things; I will put you in charge of many things. Come and share your master's happiness!" (Matthews 25:21).

Chun-Wai Chan, MD

EPILOGUE

As I look back on my life, I see many bends in the road. Some bends were the results of God's mercy and grace, and some were His correction and discipline. From a street child to a child of God, from Hong Kong to America, from waiting on tables to caring for the sick, from Virginia to California, from receiving marriage counseling to mentoring other couples, this winding path was designed by God to shape and mold me to become who I am today and to prepare me for His service tomorrow.

Different passages in the Bible illustrate how God leads and guides us, to prepare us to be an instrument of His love. Take Luke 5:1-11, for example:

> *"One day as Jesus was standing by the Lake of Gennesaret, with the people crowding around him and listening to the word of God, he saw at the water's edge two boats, left there by the fishermen, who were washing their nets.*

151

He got into one of the boats, the one belonging to Simon, and asked him to put out a little from shore. Then he sat down and taught the people from the boat. When he had finished speaking, he said to Simon, 'Put out into deep water, and let down the nets for a catch.'

Simon answered, 'Master, we've worked hard all night and haven't caught anything. But because you say so, I will let down the nets.'

When they had done so, they caught such a large number of fish that their nets began to break. So they signaled their partners in the other boat to come and help them, and they came and filled both boats so full that they began to sink.

When Simon Peter saw this, he fell at Jesus' knees and said, 'Go away from me, Lord; I am a sinful man!' For he and all his companions were astonished at the catch of fish they had taken, and so were James and John, the sons of Zebedee, Simon's partners.

Then Jesus said to Simon, 'Don't be afraid; from now on you will catch men.'

So they pulled their boats up on shore, left everything and followed him."

This passage of Scripture describes the event of Jesus calling His first disciples. It illustrates several valuable lessons about God's plans in our lives:

1. God knows our needs: When Jesus saw the two boats, He already knew the needs of the fishermen without talking to them. Yet He did not address them right away. Rather, He asked them to use their boats for His purpose.

Jesus knows our needs too. He knows our struggles while traveling through the winding paths of life. Sometimes He chooses not to address our immediate needs right away. Rather, He wants to use us in our weakness, for His purpose.

2. When we depend on ourselves, we cannot accomplish anything: When Jesus told Simon to bring the boat to deep water and put the net down to catch fish, Simon was frustrated, and he replied that, as an experienced fisherman, he had worked all night and had not caught any fish.

When we reach a sharp turn in the road, a crossroad, or a long, dark tunnel in life, we cannot see what is ahead. We may become disappointed, frustrated, depressed, or even angry because we do not know what to do next.

3. Submitting to God is the way to abundant blessings: When Simon was willing to submit to Jesus, the most unbelievable thing happened. He caught so many fish that the nets began to break.

Life is not a dead-end street. Many bends in the road are hurdles, not roadblocks. They are meant to strengthen us, not defeat us. When we are trying to make it on our own, we do not give God the opportunity to perform miracles in our lives. On the other hand, when we learn to trust God and not lean on our own understanding, God will reward us with many more abundant blessings than we could imagine.

4. Blessings are meant to be shared with others: Simon had to ask his partners to share the catch. It was much too heavy for his boat to carry alone.

God blesses us so that we can be a channel of His blessing. When we keep focusing on the blessings and not the One who blesses, sooner or later we begin to think that we are the ones who brings the blessings to fruition, not God. The moment that happens, we are glorifying ourselves instead of God. The best way to counteract this temptation is to share our blessings and not hoard them. Otherwise, sooner or later, we are going to sink.

5. God has an eternal purpose for each of our lives: Jesus told Simon to leave his vocation as a fisherman and embark on a new mission as a preacher.

When God blesses us with successes in what we do, we may think that we are all set for life. But God does not want us to be so content with blessings that we become complacent. He wants us to look beyond material wealth and build treasures in heaven, because He has an eternal purpose for each of our lives.

To know God's will, we need quiet time to reflect and reassess the purpose, meaning, and priority of our lives and to seek His will. When we are going a hundred miles an hour on this winding path of life, there is no time to seek God's will. With each bend in the road, God wants us to slow down, and even, sometimes, to be still.

Only when we are still can we see better, hear better, and think better.

Dear friend,

If we could sit down and talk, here is what I would say. As God has always had a plan for me, God has a plan for you, too. As you travel down the winding path of your life, you may encounter twists, turns, and dark tunnels. Do not be afraid. They are designed to shape and mold you to become a better person. Always trust God no matter what happens. He knows your needs. He will lead and guide you according to His timing. When you learn to totally submit to Him, He will bless you abundantly.

On the other hand, when your path is straight and smooth, do not get wrapped up in your success. God has an eternal purpose for you: to go beyond material wealth and store treasures in heaven. So when you are successful, do not go faster and faster. Slow down, listen to His voice, and seek His will. You will then understand His plan for your life.

"May the Lord bless you and keep you; the Lord make His face shine upon you and be gracious to you; the Lord turn His face toward you and give you peace" (Numbers 6:24-26).

Chun-Wai Chan, MD

Chun-Wai Chan, MD

CHILDREN'S GARDEN FOUNDATION

HISTORY:

Between 1951 and 1971, Christian Children's Fund, Inc. (CCF) assisted over 4,000 orphans in Hong Kong. Some of them have immigrated to the United States. After Rev. Mills passed away in 1996, the group pledged to carry on the legacy he left behind. With much enthusiasm and prayer, the group convened in San Jose, California, on July 13, 2000, and formed the Children's Garden Foundation.

The name is adopted from the "cottage plan project" in Hong Kong where Rev. Mills built a very large orphanage to accommodate 900 orphans from among the great influx of refugees from China. Construction began in 1952 and was completed in 1957. Significantly, the name, Children's Garden Foundation, symbolizes a refuge for children where they can be nurtured and developed into productive citizens.

MISSION:

We strive to raise the awareness of needy children in China, and to collectively provide for the healthy growth, development, and education of children otherwise lacking basic necessities. We pledge to give back to society by helping these children, one at a time.

FINANCIAL ACCOUNTABILITY:

As a tax-exempt organization, Children's Garden Foundation (CGF) follows established accounting procedures and internal control to ensure the utmost fiscal accountability. In addition, we adhere to the code of ethics of the United Nation's UNICEF Committee on Non-Governmental Organizations. We seek contributions from individuals and groups who share the same vision. Collectively, we will support reputable charitable organizations whose projects are consistent with our mission. 100 percent of a contribution is spent in sponsoring children in need. We have pledged to be good stewards of the trust of the contributors, and to assess, monitor, and work with only the most respected and financially responsible organizations to assist needy children in China.

CURRENT PROJECTS:

Partnering with Sunbeam Foundation, Hong Kong Christian Council, Chinese Christian Herald Crusade, and Future Hope Foundation, we re-build schools in economically deprived areas, and sponsor children in six orphanages in Guangdong, Guangxi, Fujian, Anhui, Henan, and Sichuan, China. These orphanages provide room and board, as well as educational assistance to the needy children. One of the orphanages is in Baiwan, Guangdong, which is one of the ten poorest rural townships in China, and the very place where Rev. Mills established his first church in China in 1936.

HELP US REACH MORE CHILDREN:

Children's Garden Foundation gratefully accepts your donation. Together, we can make a difference in this world, one child at a time. For $25 a month, or $300 a year, you can help a needy child in China to have food, shelter, and education. Contributions may be tax deductible to the extent of the tax law. Please go to www.lisah.org/cgf for more information. Checks may be made payable to "Children's Garden Foundation" and sent to Po-Wah Chiu, Treasurer, 212 Victory Circle, San Ramon, CA 94583.

Chun-Wai Chan, MD

PICTORIAL MILESTONES FROM MY JOURNEY

Snapshots of my life: The next few pages include photos from various places along the winding path that led me from my being an orphan in Hong Kong to being a physician today. May the Lord be glorified by what you see.

1951
I was born in Hong Kong, in this home in Kowloon Zai.

1957
Both my brother and father passed away. Picture was taken a year before. I am third from left, my younger brother is standing at front and my father is on my left.

Chun-Wai Chan, MD

PICTORIAL MILESTONES FROM MY JOURNEY

1959
My mother
and brother
took me to the
Faith-Love
Home.

Basketball court inside the orphanage.

PICTORIAL MILESTONES FROM MY JOURNEY

1964   I entered the seventh grade. Picture was taken when Dr. Clark, founder of CCF, visited Faith-Love. I am first from right.

1966
We established
contact with my
grandfather in the
United States.
Picture was taken
with my
stepfather and
family.
I am standing
at the back,
first from left.

Chun-Wai Chan, MD

PICTORIAL MILESTONES FROM MY JOURNEY

1969
I graduated from Bethel High School. I am the fourth from left.

Performing
at
graduation
concert.

PICTORIAL MILESTONES FROM MY JOURNEY

1969
We immigrated to the United States. This is one of the pictures I used to identify my grandfather at the airport.

1970
I re-enrolled in high school in New York. Picture was taken at Central Park, New York.

Chun-Wai Chan, MD

PICTORIAL MILESTONES FROM MY JOURNEY

1971
I entered
Princeton
University.

PICTORIAL MILESTONES FROM MY JOURNEY

Christmas
with my
grandfather
and
mother.

1975
I graduated
from
Princeton.
Picture
was taken
with Jade.

PICTORIAL MILESTONES FROM MY JOURNEY

1975
Jade
and
I
got
married.

Jade
with
her
mother.

PICTORIAL MILESTONES FROM MY JOURNEY

1975   I entered Harvard Medical School.

1976   Jade enrolled in the Physician's Assistant
Program at Northeastern University.

Chun-Wai Chan, MD

Pictorial Milestones From My Journey

1979   I graduated from Harvard with a combined MD-MPH degree. Picture was taken with Dr. Oliver Cope, pioneer of endocrine surgery, and classmate, Nancy Oriel.

1980   We reunited with Rev. and Mrs. Mills. Picture was taken a year later when our first daughter, Jamie, was born.

PICTORIAL MILESTONES FROM MY JOURNEY

1981
We reunited
with my sponsor
Doris Hawkins
(first from left).
Picture was
taken a year later
when she came
to Richmond,
Virginia, to visit
us.

1987
I went back
to cardiology
fellowship
training after
teaching in
medical
school for
five years.
Picture was
taken a year
later.

PICTORIAL MILESTONES FROM MY JOURNEY

1989   I started my career with Kaiser Permanente. Pictured here are Jamie (left), Janice (right), and Verent (middle).

1994   Mills Endowment Fund was started. Picture was taken with Rev. and Mrs. Mills at a fundraising event.

PICTORIAL MILESTONES FROM MY JOURNEY

1994   Visiting a CCF project in Mexico.

2000   Children's Garden Foundation was founded. Picture was taken during a visit to one of the orphanages we supported in China.

PICTORIAL MILESTONES FROM MY JOURNEY

2003   Jamie graduated from Princeton. Jade,
Janice, and I went to her graduation.

2007   Janice graduated from University of California, San Diego.
Family picture taken following graduation ceremony.

PICTORIAL MILESTONES FROM MY JOURNEY

2008   LISAH (Love Is Spoken At Home), a family relationship ministry, was started. Picture was taken in one of the seminars.

2009   Jamie married to Jeff Lee.

PICTORIAL MILESTONES FROM MY JOURNEY

2010   Verent graduated from California Polytech University, San Luis Obispo. Family picture taken following graduation ceremony.

Family reunion at Christmas, with Jeff joining the family.

PICTORIAL MILESTONES FROM MY JOURNEY

With Muriel and Don Strum, Rev. and Mrs. Mills'
daughter and son-in-law.

With cardiology colleagues at Kaiser, Fresno.

Chun-Wai Chan, MD

RESOURCES FROM HEALTHY LIFE PRESS

Unless otherwise noted on the site itself, shipping is free for all products purchased through *www.healthylifepress.com.*

NEW RELEASES – FALL 2014

Mommy, What's 'Died' Mean? - How the Butterfly Story Helped Little Dave Understand His Grandpa's Death, by Linda Swain Gill; Illustrated by David Lee Bass (a.k.a. "Little Dave") – Designed to assist Christian parents and other adults who love and care about children to talk with them about the difficult subject of death, the story traces a small child's experience following his grandpa's and shows how his mother sensitively answered his questions about death by using simple examples derived from the birth of a butterfly. Little Dave's story is colorfully illustrated and designed for a child and parent or trusted adult to read together. The story has been created especially for children from pre-kindergarten through 4th grade. Discussion questions are included for each story page to help determine how much the child understands. A simple imitation game is also included to help involve the child in the story. Several pages at the end of the book contain suggestions about how to discuss death and dying with children of various ages. (**Full-color printed book: $14.99; PDF eBook: $9.99; both together: $19.99** – direct from publisher; printed books and eBooks available at *www.Amazon.com; www.BN.com; www.deepershopping.com,* and wherever books are sold.)

No Worries - Spiritual and Mental Health Counseling for Anxiety, by Elaine Leong Eng, MD – Offering a unique spiritual and mental health perspective on a major malady of our age, this practicing Christian psychiatrist has packed a dose of reality mixed with medicine and faith into a book aimed at informing, inspiring, and equipping those who wish to better help those who struggle with anxiety and related disorders, both inside

and outside the church. As one endorser said, "I travel all over the world. I see fellow believers suffering from different forms of anxiety and worry. Dr. Eng's book gives me tools to recognize when people are suffering and how to encourage them to get the help they need." (Printed book: $19.99; PDF eBook: $9.99; both together: $24.99 – direct from publisher; printed books and eBooks available at *www.Amazon.com*; *www.BN. com*; *www.deepershopping.com*, and wherever books are sold.)

 **If God Is So Good, Why Do I Hurt So Bad?**, by David B. Biebel, DMin – This **25th Anniversary Edition** of a best-selling classic (over 200,000 copies in print worldwide, in a dozen languages) is the book's first major revision since its initial release in 1989. This new version features additional original material related to the conundrum of suffering and faith (with principles learned along the way), and chapter ending questions for personal or group use. Endorser Sheila Walsh wrote, "I believe this is one of the most profound, empathetic and beautiful books ever written on the subject of suffering and loss. There is no attempt to quickly ease our pain but rather, with an understanding born in the crucible God uniquely designed for him, David offers a place to stand, a place to fall and a place to rise again. This book left an indelible mark on my heart over twenty years ago and now with this new release the gift is fresh and fragrant. I highly commend this to you!" (Printed book: $14.99; PDF eBook: $9.99; both together: $19.95 – direct from publisher; printed books and eBooks available at *www.Amazon.com*; *www.BN.com*; *www. deepershopping.com*, and wherever books are sold.)

Earlier Releases

 **We've Got Mail: The New Testament Letters in Modern English – As Relevant Today as Ever!** by Rev. Warren C. Biebel, Jr. – A modern English paraphrase of the New Testament Letters, sure to inspire in readers a loving appreciation for God's Word. (Printed book: $9.95; PDF eBook: $6.95; both together: $15.00 – direct from publisher; printed books and eBooks available at *www.Amazon.com*; *www.BN.com*; *www.deepershopping. com*, and wherever books are sold.)

Hearth & Home – Recipes for Life, by Karey Swan (7th Edition) – Far more than a cookbook, this classic is a life book, with recipes for life as well as for great food. Karey describes how to buy and prepare from scratch a wide variety of tantalizing dishes, while weaving into the book's fabric the wisdom of the ages plus the recipe that she and her husband used to raise their kids. A great gift for Christmas or for a new bride. (Perfect Bound book [8 x 10, glossy cover]: $17.95; PDF eBook: $12.95; both together: $24.95 – direct from publisher; printed books and eBooks available at *www.Amazon.com*; *www.BN.com*; *www.deepershopping.com*, and wherever books are sold.)

Who Me, Pray? Prayer 101: Praying Aloud, for Beginners, by Gary A. Burlingame – Who Me, Pray? is a practical guide for prayer, based on Jesus' direction in "The Lord's Prayer," with examples provided for use in typical situations where you might be asked or expected to pray in public. (Printed book: $6.95; PDF eBook: $2.99; both together: $7.95 – direct from publisher; printed books and eBooks available at *www.Amazon.com*; *www.BN. com*; *www.deepershopping.com*, and wherever books are sold.)

My Broken Heart Sings, the poetry of Gary Burlingame – In 1987, Gary and his wife Debbie lost their son Christopher John, at only six months of age, to a chronic lung disease. This life-changing experience gave them a special heart for helping others through similar loss and pain. (Printed book: $10.95; PDF eBook: $6.95; both together: $13.95 – direct from publisher; printed books and eBooks available at *www.Amazon.com*; *www. BN.com*; *www.deepershopping.com*, and wherever books are sold.)

After Normal: One Teen's Journey Following Her Brother's Death, by Diane Aggen – Based on a journal the author kept following her younger brother's death. It offers helpful insights and understanding for teens facing a similar loss or for those who might wish to understand and help teens facing a similar loss. (Printed book: $11.95; PDF eBook: $6.95; both together: $15.00 – direct from publisher; printed books and eBooks

available at *www.Amazon.com*; *www.BN.com*; *www.deepershopping.com*, and wherever books are sold.)

In the Unlikely Event of a Water Landing – Lessons Learned from Landing in the Hudson River, by Andrew Jamison, MD – The author was flying standby on US Airways Flight 1549 toward Charlotte on January 15, 2009, from New York City, where he had been interviewing for a residency position. Little did he know that the next stop would be the Hudson River. Riveting and inspirational, this book would be especially helpful for people in need of hope and encouragement. (Printed book: $8.95; PDF eBook: $6.95; both together: $12.95 – direct from publisher; printed books and eBooks available at *www.Amazon.com*; *www.BN.com*; *www.deepershopping.com*, and wherever books are sold.)

Finding Martians in the Dark – Everything I Needed to Know About Teaching Took Me Only 30 Years to Learn, by Dan M. Biebel – Packed with wise advice based on hard experience, and laced with humor, this book is a perfect teacher's gift year-round. Susan J. Wegmann, PhD, says, "Biebel's sardonic wit is mellowed by a genuine love for kids and teaching. . . . A Whitman-like sensibility flows through his stories of teaching, learning, and life."

(Printed book: $10.95; PDF eBook: $6.95; Together: $15.00 – direct from publisher; printed books and eBooks available at *www.Amazon.com*; *www.BN.com*; *www.deepershopping.com*, and wherever books are sold.)

Because We're Family and **Because We're Friends,** by Gary A. Burlingame – Sometimes things related to faith can be hard to discuss with your family and friends. These booklets are designed to be given as gifts, to help you open the door to discussing spiritual matters with family members and friends who are open to such a conversation. (Printed book: $5.95 each; PDF eBook: $4.95 each; both together: $9.95 [printed & eBook of the same title] – direct from publisher; printed books and eBooks available at *www.Amazon.com*; *www.BN.com*; *www.deepershopping.com*, and wherever books are sold.)

The Transforming Power of Story: How Telling Your Story Brings Hope to Others and Healing to Yourself, by Elaine Leong Eng, MD, and David B. Biebel, DMin – This book demonstrates, through multiple true life stories, how sharing one's story, especially in a group setting, can bring hope to listeners and healing to the one who shares. Individuals facing difficulties will find this book greatly encouraging. (Printed book: $14.99; PDF eBook: $9.99; both together: $19.99 – direct from publisher; printed books and eBooks available at *www.Amazon.com*; *www.BN.com*; *www.deepershopping.com*, and wherever books are sold.)

You Deserved a Better Father: Good Parenting Takes a Plan, by Robb Brandt, MD – About parenting by intention, and other lessons the author learned through the loss of his firstborn son. It is especially for parents who believe that bits and pieces of leftover time will be enough for their own children. (Printed book: $12.95 each; PDF eBook: $6.95; both together: $17.95 – direct from publisher; printed books and eBooks available at

www.Amazon.com; *www.BN.com*; *www.deepershopping.com*, and wherever books are sold.)

eBook Cover

Printed Cover

Jonathan, You Left Too Soon, by David B. Biebel, DMin – One pastor's journey through the loss of his son, into the darkness of depression, and back into the light of joy again, emerging with a renewed sense of mission. (Printed book: $12.95; PDF eBook: $5.99; both together: $15.00 – direct from publisher; printed books and eBooks available at *www.Amazon.com*; *www.BN.com*; *www.deepershopping. com*, and wherever books are sold.)

Unless otherwise noted on the site itself, shipping is free for all products purchased through <u>www.healthylifepress.com</u>.

The Spiritual Fitness Checkup for the 50-Something Woman, by Sharon V. King, PhD – Following the stages of a routine medical exam, the author describes ten spiritual fitness "checkups" midlife women can conduct to assess their spiritual health and tone up their relationship with God. Each checkup consists of the author's personal reflections, a Scripture reference for meditation, and a "Spiritual Pulse Check," with exercises readers can use for personal application. (Printed book: $8.95; PDF eBook: $6.95; both together: $12.95 – direct from publisher; printed books and eBooks available at *www.Amazon.com*; *www.BN.com*; *www.deepershopping.com*, and wherever books are sold.)

The Other Side of Life – Over 60? God Still Has a Plan for You, by Rev. Warren C. Biebel, Jr. – Drawing on biblical examples and his 60-plus years of pastoral experience, Rev. Biebel helps older (and younger) adults understand God's view of aging and the rich life available to everyone who seeks a deeper relationship with God as they age. Rev. Biebel explains how to: Identify God's ongoing plan for your life; Rely on faith to manage the anxieties of aging;

Form positive, supportive relationships; Cultivate patience; Cope with new technologies; Develop spiritual integrity; Understand the effects of dementia; Develop a Christ-centered perspective of aging. (Printed book: $10.95; PDF eBook: $6.95; both together: $15.00 – direct from publisher; printed books and eBooks available at *www.Amazon.com*; *www.BN.com*; *www.deepershopping.com*, and wherever books are sold.)

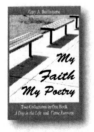

My Faith, My Poetry, by Gary A. Burlingame – This unique book of Christian poetry is actually two in one. The first collection of poems, A Day in the Life, explores a working parent's daily journey of faith. The reader is carried from morning to bedtime, from "In the Details," to "I Forgot to Pray," back to "Home Base," and finally to "Eternal Love Divine." The second collection of poems, Come Running, is wonder, joy, and faith wrapped up in words that encourage and inspire the mind and the heart. (Printed book: $10.95; PDF eBook: $6.95; both together: $13.95 – direct from publisher; printed books and eBooks available at *www.Amazon.com*; *www.BN.com*; *www.deepershopping.com*, and wherever books are sold.)

On Eagles' Wings, by Sara Eggleston – One woman's life journey from idyllic through chaotic to joy, carried all the way by the One who has promised to never leave us nor forsake us. Remarkable, poignant, moving, and inspiring, this autobiographical account will help many who are facing difficulties that seem too great to overcome or even bear at all. It is proof that Isaiah 40:31 is as true today as when it was penned, "But they that wait upon the LORD shall renew their strength; they shall mount up with wings as eagles; they shall run, and not be weary; and they shall walk, and not faint." (Printed book: $14.95; PDF eBook: $8.95; both together: $22.95 – direct from publisher; printed books and eBooks available at *www.Amazon.com*; *www.BN.com*; *www.deepershopping.com*, and wherever books are sold.)

Richer Descriptions, by Gary A. Burlingame – A unique and handy manual, covering all nine human senses in seven chapters, for Christian speakers and writers. Exercises and a speaker's checklist equip speakers to engage their audiences in a richer experience. Writing examples and a writer's guide help writers bring more life to the characters and scenes of their stories. Bible references encourage a deeper appreciation of being created by God

for a sensory existence. (Printed book: $15.95; PDF eBook: $8.95; both together: $22.95 – direct from publisher; printed books and eBooks available at *www.Amazon.com*; *www.BN.com*; *www.deepershopping.com*, and wherever books are sold.)

Treasuring Grace, by Rob Plumley and Tracy Roberts – This novel was inspired by a dream. Liz Swanson's life isn't quite what she'd imagined, but she considers herself lucky. She has a good husband, beautiful children, and fulfillment outside of her home through volunteer work. On some days she doesn't even notice the dull ache in her heart. While she's preparing for their summer kickoff at Lake George, the ache disappears and her sudden happiness is mistaken for anticipation of their weekend. However, as the family heads north, there are clouds on the horizon that have nothing to do with the weather. Only Liz's daughter, who's found some of her mother's hidden journals, has any idea what's wrong. But by the end of the weekend, there will be no escaping the truth or its painful buried secrets.

(Printed: $12.95; PDF eBook: $7.95; both together: $19.95 – direct from publisher; printed books and eBooks available at *www.Amazon.com*; *www.BN.com*; *www.deepershopping.com*, and wherever books are sold.)

From Orphan to Physician – The Winding Path, by Chun-Wai Chan, MD – From the foreword: "In this book, Dr. Chan describes how his family escaped to Hong Kong, how they survived in utter poverty, and how he went from being an orphan to graduating from Harvard Medical School and becoming a cardiologist. The writing is fluent, easy to read and understand. The sequence of events is realistic, emotionally moving, spiritually touching, heartwarming, and thought provoking. The book illustrates . . . how one must have faith in order to walk through life's winding path." (Printed book: $14.95; PDF eBook: $8.95; both together: $22.95 – direct from publisher; printed books and eBooks available at *www.Amazon.com*; *www.BN.com*; *www.deepershopping.com*, and wherever books are sold.)

12 Parables, by Wayne Faust – Timeless Christian stories about doubt, fear, change, grief, and more. Using tight, entertaining prose, professional musician and comedy performer Wayne Faust manages to deal with difficult concepts in a simple, straightforward way. These are stories you can read aloud over and over—to your spouse, your family, or in a group setting. Packed with emotion and just enough mystery to keep you wondering, while

providing lots of points to ponder and discuss when you're through, these stories relate the gospel in the tradition of the greatest speaker of parables the world has ever known, who appears in them often. (Printed book: $14.95; PDF eBook: $8.95; both together: $22.95 – direct from publisher; printed books and eBooks available at *www.Amazon.com*; *www.BN.com*; *www.deepershopping.com*, and wherever books are sold.)

The Answer is Always "Jesus," by Aram Haroutunian, who gave children's sermons for 15 years at a large church in Golden, Colorado—well over 500 in all. This book contains 74 of his most unforgettable presentations—due to the children's responses. Pastors, homeschoolers, parents who often lead family devotions, or other storytellers will find these stories, along with comments about props and how to prepare and present them, an invaluable asset in reconnecting with the simplest, most profound truths of Scripture, and then to envision how best to communicate these so even a child can understand them. (Printed book: $12.95; PDF eBook: $8.95; both together: $19.95 – direct from publisher; printed books and eBooks available at *www.Amazon.com*; *www.BN.com*; *www.deepershopping.com*, and wherever books are sold.)

 **Handbook of Faith**, by Rev. Warren C. Biebel, Jr. – The New York Times World 2011 Almanac claimed that there are 2 billion, 200 thousand Christians in the world, with "Christians" being defined as "followers of Christ." The original 12 followers of Christ changed the world; indeed, they changed the history of the world. So this author, a pastor with over 60 years' experience, poses and answers this logical question: "If there are so many 'Christians' on this planet, why are they so relatively ineffective in serving the One they claim to follow?" Answer: Because, unlike Him, they do not know and trust the Scriptures, implicitly. This little volume will help you do that. (Printed book: $8.95; PDF eBook: $6.95; both together: $13.95 – direct from publisher; printed books and eBooks available at *www.Amazon.com*; *www.BN.com*; *www.deepershopping.com*, and wherever books are sold.)

Pieces of My Heart, by David L. Wood – Eighty-two lessons from normal everyday life. David's hope is that these stories will spark thoughts about God's constant involvement and intervention in our lives and stir a sense of how much He cares about every detail that is important to us. The piece missing represents his son, Daniel, who died in a fire shortly before his first birthday. (Printed book: $16.95; PDF eBook: $8.95; both together: $24.95 – direct from publisher; printed books and eBooks available at *www.Amazon.com*; *www.BN.com*; *www.deepershopping.com*, and wherever books are sold.)

Unless otherwise noted on the site itself, shipping is free for all products purchased through www.healthylifepress.com.

Dream House, by Justa Carpenter – Written by a New England builder of several hundred homes, the idea for this book came to him one day as he was driving that came to him one day as was driving from one job site to another. He pulled over and recorded it so he would remember it, and now you will remember it, too, if you believe, as he does, that "... He who has begun a good work in you will complete it until the day of Jesus Christ." (Printed book: $10.95; PDF eBook: $6.95; both together: $13.95 – direct from publisher; printed books and eBooks available at *www.Amazon.com*; *www.BN.com*; *www.deepershopping.com*, and wherever books are sold.)

A Simply Homemade Clean, by homesteader Lisa Barthuly – "Somewhere along the path, it seems we've lost our gumption, the desire to make things ourselves," says the author. "Gone are the days of 'do it yourself.' Really . . . why bother? There are a slew of retailers just waiting for us with anything and everything we could need; packaged up all pretty, with no thought or effort required. It is the manifestation of 'progress' . . . right?" I don't buy that!" Instead, Lisa describes how to make safe and effective cleansers for home, laundry, and body right in your own home. This saves money and avoids exposure to harmful chemicals often found in commercially produced cleansers. (**Full-color** printed book: $16.99; PDF eBook: $6.95; both together: $22.95 – direct from publisher; printed books and eBooks available at *www.Amazon.com*; *www.BN.com*; *www.deepershopping.com*, and wherever books are sold.)

The Secret of Singing Springs, by Monte Swan – One Colorado family's treasure-hunting adventure along the trail of Jesse James. The Secret of Singing Springs is written to capture for children and their parents the spirit of the hunt—the hunt for treasure as in God's Truth, which is the objective of walking the Way of Wisdom that is described in Proverbs. (Printed book: $12.95, PDF eBook: $9.99; both together: $19.99 – direct from publisher; printed books and eBooks available at *www.Amazon.com*; *www.BN.com*; *www.deepershopping.com*, and wherever books are sold.)

God Loves You Circle, by Michelle Johnson – Daily inspiration for your deeper walk with Christ. This collection of short stories of Christian living will make you laugh, make you cry, but most of all make you contemplate—the meaning and value of walking with the Master moment-by-moment, day-by-day. (**Full-color** printed book: $17.95; PDF eBook: $9.99; both together: $22.99 – direct from publisher; printed books and eBooks available at *www.Amazon.com*; *www.BN.com*; *www.deepershopping.com*, and wherever books are sold.)

Our God-Given Senses, by Gary A. Burlingame – Did you know humans have NINE senses? The Bible draws on these senses to reveal spiritual truth. We are to taste and see that the Lord is a good. We are to carry the fragrance of Christ. Our faith is produced upon hearing. Jesus asked Thomas to touch him. God created us for a sensory experience and that is what you will find in this book. (Printed book: $12.99; PDF eBook: $9.99; both together: $19.99 – direct from publisher; printed books and eBooks available at *www.Amazon.com*; *www.BN.com*; *www.deepershopping.com*, and wherever books are sold.)

Vows, a Romantic novel by F. F. Whitestone – When the police cruiser pulled up to the curb outside, Faith Framingham's heart skipped a beat, for she could see that Chuck, who should have been driving, was not in the vehicle. Chuck's partner, Sandy, stepped out slowly. Sandy's pursed lips and ashen face spoke volumes. Faith waited by the front door, her hands clasped tightly, to counter the fact that her mind was already reeling. "Love never fails." A compelling story. (Printed book: $12.99; PDF eBook: $9.99; both together, $19.99 – direct from publisher; printed books and eBooks available at *www.Amazon.com*; *www.BN.com*; *www.deepershopping.com*, and wherever books are sold.)

Unless otherwise noted on the site itself, shipping is free for all products purchased through www.healthylifepress.com.

Worth the Cost?, by Jack Tsai, MD – The author was happily on his way to obtaining the American Dream until he decided to take seriously Jesus' command, "Come, follow me." Join him as he explores the cost of medical education and Christian discipleship. Planning to serve God in your future vocation? Take care that your desires do not get side-tracked by the false promises of this world. What you should be doing now so when you are done with your training you will still want to serve God. (Printed book: $12.99, PDF eBook: $9.99; both together: $19.99 – direct from publisher; printed books and eBooks available at *www.Amazon.com*; *www.BN.com*; *www.deepershopping.com*, and wherever books are sold.)

Nature: God's Second Book – An Essential Link to Restoring Your Personal Health and Wellness: Body, Mind, and Spirit, by Elvy P. Rolle – An inspirational book that looks at nature across the seasons of nature and of life. It uses the biblical Emmaus Journey as an analogy for life's journey, and offers ideas for using nature appreciation and exploration to reduce life's stresses. The author shares her personal story of how she came to grips with this concept after three trips to the emergency room. (**Full-color** printed book: $12.99; PDF eBook $8.99; both together: $16.99 – direct from publisher; printed books and eBooks available at *www.Amazon.com*; *www.BN.com*; *www.deepershopping.com*, and wherever books are sold.)

He Waited, by LaDonna Cooper – Inspires readers to wait upon the Lord for His best for them; stresses the importance of putting God's purpose above one's own; emphasizes that God's love is unconditional; demonstrates the wisdom of waiting, through a combination of positive insights, encouragement, biblical examples and principles. Decorated with original poetry by the author. For singles and others who are waiting. Distributed primarily through *www.Amazon.com*. (Printed book: $10.99; PDF eBook: $9.99; both together: $15.99 – direct from publisher; printed books and eBooks available at *www.Amazon.com*; *www.BN.com*; *www.deepershopping.com*, and wherever books are sold.)

SEASONAL

 The Big Black Book – What the Christmas Tree Saw, by Rev. Warren C. Biebel, Jr. – An original Christmas story, from the perspective of the Christmas tree. This little book is especially suitable for parents to read to their children at Christmas time or all year-round. (**Full-color** printed book: $9.95; PDF eBook: $4.95; both together: $12.95 – direct from publisher; printed books and eBooks available at *www.Amazon.com*; *www.BN.com*; *www.deepershopping.com*, and wherever books are sold.)

CPSIA information can be obtained
at www.ICGtesting.com
Printed in the USA
FFOW02n1304020118
44319827-43949FF